Once I Was Blind But Now I See

By Charles Piccirilli

With Kimberly Cook

D1518412

Published by Spiritu Sancto Press
403L Aggies Circle, Unit L, Bel Air, MD 21014
info@spiritusanctopress.com

Cover design by Micah Piccirilli / Cover photo by Bruce Weller

FORWARD

By Monsignor Kevin T. Schenning

Charles Piccirilli came to me about twenty years ago seeking spiritual direction. At that time I was pastor of St. Joan of Arc Catholic Church in Aberdeen, MD. Our school secretary, Dru Blackburn, recommended me to Charles. Dru was a close friend of Charles and knew he was looking for spiritual direction. She felt strongly that the two of us would be a good fit.

When I first met Charles in 1997, I saw right away a holy and genuine man. He was enthusiastic about his faith, desired obedience to the Church, and was seeking the will of God in all things. As Charles shared deeper the ways in which God was communicating with him throughout his life, I felt that I had a clear understanding of his relationship with the Lord. We connected immediately and it has been refreshing to help guide him along his spiritual journey.

He and his family have continued to serve throughout these twenty years in any way they are able. This has included participating in a Life in the Spirit seminar at St. Joan of Arc parish, of which chapter twenty in this book testifies. At my request in 2006, as Pastor at St. Joseph in Fullerton, Charles helped to lead another seminar there. In 2009 Charles asked me to become the spiritual director for a young adult group he had formed called Straight Forward, and I learned of the many fruits born to those young people.

For Charles, the years have been truly filled with blessings, and yet not devoid of turbulence. Charles has struggled to battle past demons and put to rest his own moments of anxiety and depression. In him, I have come to know a man who takes every obstacle given him in the true name of Christianity–from death to resurrection. Charles manages to see all suffering through the eyes of the cross, in which Christ always prevails victorious.

PREFACE

By Kimberly Cook

Why is it that I felt so compelled to help with this project?
Why the very need to get this book into the hands of those whose
lives surely will be changed in the hearing of its truth?

It's because I too was changed by the events in this book, and
I mean radically changed. I too was once blind. Thereafter and
for many years since, I have been thankful to witness some of
the miraculous works of God recorded in these pages, and I have
known some of the named persons quite well.

God truly has blessed Charles Piccirilli with a great gift of faith,
and Charles has shared that gift abundantly. I have come to
refer to him affectionately as *"my personal Padre Pio,"* and after
reading his journey with God, I believe you will know why.

This is Charles' story—it tells how our Lord speaks to an ordinary
man—a sinner just like you and me—and through him, he does
wondrous things for those who trust in his word.

INTRODUCTION

By Charles Piccirilli

Christian Witness

This book gives witness to the power of Jesus Christ through the Holy Spirit. It is my personal witness to the incredible things he has done in my life, and continues to do, through my regular encounters with him.

In addition to what has happed in my own life experiences, I also am documenting the personal experiences of many other individuals. This is all to give glory to God, in the hope that these testimonies may encourage others who are seeking a deeper relationship with the Lord.

You too may have heard God's voice, or perhaps you have witnessed his mercy and love through his miracles in your life. If you have not, please say a prayer right now, and ask the Holy Spirit to open your eyes and your heart as you read on. And as you read, may you know that God truly desires to reveal himself to you, to speak to you, and to have a deep personal relationship with you. As a Catholic, I am thankful for the teachings of Christ, interpreted through his Church, which have been clear since the very beginning.

The Desire for God

Catechism of the Catholic Church #27
"The desire for God is written in the human heart, because man is created by God and for God; and God never ceases to draw man to himself. Only in God will he find the truth and happiness he never stops searching for: The dignity of man rests above all on the fact that he is called to communion with God. This invitation to converse with God is addressed to man as soon as he comes into being. For if man exists it is because God has created him through love, and through love continues to hold him in existence. He cannot live fully according to truth unless he freely acknowledges that love and entrusts himself to his creator."

"I am the good shepherd; I know my own and my own know me, as the Father knows me and I know the Father; and I lay down my life for the sheep. And I have other sheep that are not of this fold; I must bring them also, and they will heed my voice. So there shall be one flock, one shepherd."

John 10:14-16

CONTENTS

PART ONE:

Once
I Was
Blind

CHAPTER ONE

My History of Doubt & Despair

As a young boy, just like many other boys, I had dreams of flying and thoughts of Superman. The sweet innocence of my youth preserved in me a blind trust that I didn't know could be lost. I felt safe and very loved by my large, Catholic, Italian family. It was a time when nothing frightened me, when the love of God surrounding me was unexplainable and unquestionable.

When I was five, my father was in the military, and he was my hero. I remember how I longed for him to come home whenever he was away. My older brother Bud would often play jokes on me, saying, "Look, Daddy's coming down the street!" I would run excitedly to the window with great expectation, overjoyed to finally see my dad as he approached.

I fell for Bud's joke every time, my face dropping as I saw nothing but an empty road outside the window. The disappointed look and tears on my face would send my brother into hysterics.

Bud had no idea how jarring his innocent childhood jokes were for me, or that I would carry the fallout of some of them into adulthood. He was just doing what an older brother does, not understanding that a passing comment or thoughtless action could shake me to my core, causing me to question everything upon which I had built my security.

Then, one night, Bud's teasing opened Pandora's box.

"Go to sleep, boys," my mother had called down the hallway to us as we climbed into our bunk beds. Bud scaled the ladder to the "privileged" top bunk, where he would often lean over to say things to me. I hopped into the bottom bunk and slid under my covers. As the lights went out and sleep began drifting in, my brother leaned over and stated quite seriously, "Charles, you are going to die."

My eyes shot back open, and suddenly I was fully alert. "What did he say?" I thought. "I am going to die? What does he mean by that, and more importantly...is it true?"

It was at that moment that doubt and terror entered my life for the very first time. I was going to die! Maybe not today or tomorrow, or even next week, but someday I would die.

In that one cold and sobering instant, I was made aware of my mortality. Part of my innocence had been shattered that night by the realization that I was not immortal. I could not fly, there was no Superman, and one day I would cease to exist. That seed of doubt planted within me began to grow, as did fear and mistrust. I would never be quite the same again. Not long after that defining moment in my life, my body began to assure me of my mortality and guaranteed expiration. I became very sick, unable to keep food in my little body. Even after I spent almost five months at Johns Hopkins Hospital, the doctors were unable to identify the source of my continuing illness. That once fearless five-year-old boy became skin and bones, being fed through needles and quickly losing hope. I still remember the day my mother and father finally came to get me and take me home. I happily climbed into our comfortable old car as joy and relief washed over me. What a glorious sight it was to see our house come into view through the side window of the back seat in the car.

The whole family was there to greet me, and we had quite a celebration that night. It's funny how I can still see us all gathered

around a big cake that was made just for me, and how excited
I felt over a small plastic wallet I received as a gift.

That overwhelming happiness was short-lived, however;
my parents were only preparing me for a transition to a more
permanent children's convalescent home named Happy Hills
which was anything but happy to me.

At Happy Hills, Dad and Mom explained, the doctors and nurses
could monitor me around the clock, ensuring that I would gain
weight and regain my health. I would live there indefinitely,
along with other sick children, receiving the proper, specialized
care I needed.

I went most unwillingly to that home, and my reluctance
manifested itself into physical and emotional realities over the
course of the next several months. Two major changes occurred.

First, I began to sweat so profusely that my clothes had to be
changed three or four times a day. This excessive sweating has
continued to this day. The second was an emotional change,
through which I encountered a deep sense of abandonment.
My parents had left me alone in a strange place, which was
neither comfortable nor welcoming. Worse than that, I quickly
realized, I was a burden.

All the children at the home slept together in one very large room.
Our cots were just two or three feet apart. On my first night,
I woke up and had to go to the bathroom, a constant reminder
of my illness. The other children were all sleeping, and I was too
weak to make it to the bathroom on my own. I called to one of the
nurses, who had to go with me.

The first few times this occurred, the nurse went willingly. As it
continued to happen throughout the night, however, she became
increasingly annoyed and impatient with me. Finally, she said,
"That's it! I am not doing this all night." She placed a pot and a

towel on the floor next to my cot, barking, "When you have to go, use this pot." Then she turned and walked away.

Deep fear and despair came over me. I felt a darkness I never had experienced before. A window to a cold and uncaring world had been opened, and my exposure to it continued throughout the humiliation those nurses caused during my illness. From that point on, I refused to use the pot next to my cot, painfully holding it in until I was alone and could sneak to the bathroom. I stopped reaching out and expecting kindness from anyone there. Goodness seemed to be fleeting, as the light within me continued to dim.

The cruelness I encountered during my treatment at Happy Hills, my sense of abandonment, and the memory of my brother's haunting words from the top bunk led me to believe that I was the only person I could trust.

As I grew older, I held onto this mentality, and I became a very self-reliant young man. I didn't need or trust anyone else. The chip on my shoulder also wore me down throughout the years. I experienced a growing and unexplainable need for something more than myself–something more than all of us. I was gasping for air outside my own bubble, which spurred my incredible pursuit to find some real evidence for the existence (or lack of existence) of God.

You would think that by seeking something as great and glorious as God, I would grow into a loving and trusting man. Instead, I became prideful and bitter, and I turned my focus in on myself rather than on the voice of truth. I became a staunch critic of faith, championing my superior intellect and my overall lack of need for a savior. I was going to save myself.

My father, the man I loved most, had developed an obsession with the occult. I followed him willingly in his search for something more, which eventually ensured that I completely abandoned the Catholic beliefs my mother had so firmly instilled in me.

I remember the exact day I closed the door on my practice of Catholicism. I was fourteen years old, and Easter was drawing near. Mom insisted (as she always did) that we go to church and receive the sacrament of Penance in preparation for Easter. This wasn't the worst thing she could have asked, because the priest at our parish knew me well, and I felt comfortable talking with him.

I kneeled casually in the confessional and rattled off a few trivial sins. Then, having done my due diligence, I sat there and waited for the standard absolution.

To my shock, Father calmly admonished, "I do not forgive you." I paused for a few awkward moments, with eyebrows raised, trying in vain to see Father's expression through the screen. I wondered if this was a joke, and he would burst out laughing at any moment. But instead, he said, "I do not forgive you, because you are not really asking for forgiveness. You just want to please your mother by receiving Easter communion."

I couldn't believe it! "Could he really do this?" I wondered as I sat dumbfounded. After a long silence, he finally continued, "If you really want to receive communion, come back to confession for six weeks straight, and I will forgive you."

I walked home in a daze, disgusted with the fact that I was not absolved and furious about the challenge he had laid before me. When I told my mother what the priest had said to me, she responded indifferently with a shrug of her shoulders. "He's just a man. Go to someone else."

How could she just dismiss it like that? After all, she was the one who had insisted I go in the first place. I didn't know much about the priesthood or the sacraments, but if there was one thing I did know, it was that confession was not about shopping around for the "right" priest to forgive my sins.

As my pride and stubbornness swelled, I was determined not to let this go. I would not go to anyone else.

Out of sheer spite, I returned week after week to that same confessional, facing Father on the other side of the screen. After the sixth week, having finally proven myself, Father absolved me of my sins. I had met the challenge, I had shown Father what I was made of, and by the way, I vowed that I was never coming back!

I sauntered down the aisle, out the front door of the church, and said definitively, "see you later" to the institution of faith altogether. From that point on, I decided, I would seek God outside of any organized religion. This prodigal son was set to roam.

It wasn't until a much later reflection that I finally was able to understand the priest's love for me through his harsh penance. He knew me, and like any good father, his tough love was meant to form me.

With the Church in the distance, I continued on my dark journey alone. I became even more self-focused, angry, and devoid of truth. On top of all that, for some unexplained reason, I began to seek other religious experiences to replace my Catholic beliefs. Although conflicted by my dabbling in the occult and my father's teachings, I still wasn't ready to stop searching for divine and supernatural answers. I turned to just about everything trying to find them.

I like to describe myself during this time as being like jello—I couldn't be nailed down to anything. I was all over the place, exploring Hinduism, Yoga, and Krishna, and then I went down the rabbit hole of the occult. Intrigued by knowledge of the hidden or paranormal, I embraced Western esotericism with arms wide open. I joined the Rosicrucian Society and Theosophical Society; engaged in transcendental meditation, astral projection, and séances; tried Ouija boards and crystal balls; and experimented with so much more. Who knows what I was opening myself up to during this time? Every door I tried was open, and yet none fulfilled my need.

Despite years of searching, I found no proof of God's existence, nor did I see signs of his presence. I was intrigued by the claims of those involved in the various dark practices, of their ability to connect with the other side. Infuriated, I tried in vain to find truth in many of their claims, but in the end, none convinced me. I did not know, love, or even have a glimmer of the presence of God.

I knew I would never be convinced until I saw and experienced the great power of God for myself. Looking back on my journey, I can see why I had no revelation of God's existence during those years.

Yes, I was searching, but I was looking in all the wrong places. The path I was on actually led me further from the God who was waiting for me. I could not see it then, but I surely was reaping a bad harvest.

My life became much worse, and the deep fear within me grew until it was all consuming. Wanting the world to know I was tough, I became a violent person and gravitated toward peers who spoke the language of violence. I began smoking and gambling, and I eventually joined a gang. I became a four-pack-a-day, dark, and angry man, full of hate and lust.

To say that I didn't have access to God or his love would be a lie. My very generous and loving family surrounded me, and I did love and honor them. Yet, my heart was closed to the true love I was longing for, and I was unreceptive to it anyway.

I often doubted the sincerity of the kind words spoken by others, assuming they were disingenuous. I knew who I was, and I didn't like myself. So, disillusioned at this point, I concluded love could not be found.

And then there was Mary.

CHAPTER TWO

First Spiritual Breakthrough

My family was very talented, and everyone strongly urged my brother Bud and me to become entertainers. I always loved my mother's sweet singing voice, and I was thankful to have gotten the gift of voice from her. With Bud's dancing talent and my voice, we gave it a shot and began performing on local Baltimore TV shows, in clubs, and at fairs.

I loved it. Performing in front of all those people made me feel important–that I had value. But after Bud tore his cartilage during one of our charity acts, I fearfully considered what the end of his dancing career meant for us.

Thankfully we regrouped and became a singing duo instead. For the next five to seven years, Bud and I took our act from Maryland all the way to the Hollywood big leagues.

But as many others have found before us, all that glitters is not gold. Three months into the Hollywood lifestyle of clubs and contracts, I realized that I hated the shallow life of Tinseltown. Nothing was real, and I desperately needed some sense of reality in my life.

Finally, returning to Maryland, I put music behind me and joined the Naval Reserve. Talk about a lifestyle change! I went from one extreme to the other, from a life on stage to a life in uniform. Through it all, my search for God continued.

My first spiritual breakthrough came shortly after I returned home from the Naval reserve. My grandpop had purchased a table of tickets for an Italian banquet in our old neighborhood, and the whole family was expected to be there. You see, in our big Italian family, we all celebrated events together–Sunday meals, holidays, funerals, card games, and basically anything the family deemed was important. One person's business was the whole family's business, and nothing went unknown by all.

Grandpop not only wanted Bud and me to be there, but he also insisted that we bring dates. "Dates?" I questioned in panic. Dating was a foreign concept to me, because I had been wrapped up in nothing but my music career and Navy life. It suddenly occurred to me that I didn't even know a girl I could ask on an actual date. I tried to imagine myself showing up at a girl's house with my goofy, bald, military 'do, but the whole idea of it made me nauseous.

That wasn't an excuse for Mom though. Oh no! She knew someone I could ask. There was a nice Italian girl named Mary, the youngest daughter of Lou and Doris Longo. They were friends who played cards each week with Mom and Dad. Mary was Mom's perfect solution.

"Mary?" I asked incredulously. "You want me to ask Mary?" I asked again, just to be sure I had heard her correctly. "That goofy girl who laughs at everything?" Then, with staunch disapproval, I said, "No way, I don't even like her. Plus, she has a boyfriend." That should have settled it, but not for my mother. So being the obedient son I was, I soon found myself dialing her number.

As if it wasn't awkward enough calling Mary to ask her for a date, I was sure she could hear my mother's voice prodding in the background while I was on the phone. "Ask her if she has a friend to go with your brother." It's true what they say about Italian mothers, or at least about my Italian mother–they really have no shame. And being the good Italian son I was, I couldn't say no to my mother, at least without the risk of being hit by a flying slipper! Mary quickly put me out of my misery by agreeing to go, and offering to invite her friend Pauline as a date for my brother.

So there we were, Bud and I, the travelling performers, stripped of all confidence as we dressed ourselves up and nervously went to pick up our dates. Of course we did so with a happy and smiling mother to see us off.

Bud drove and Pauline sat in front with him. I found myself sitting uncomfortably in the back seat next to Mary, staring out my window. I kept asking myself, "What in the world am I doing?"

I didn't want to sit too close to her for fear she might get the wrong idea. And I was sure as soon as she got close enough to look at my hair, she would start with her loud and obnoxious laughter. But to my surprise, Mary was very quiet on that ride. I sneaked a side peek at her and again asked myself, "Why am I doing this? I don't even like this girl?" The whole arrangement was unnerving.

God certainly chooses unlikely moments to communicate with us that are as mysterious as he is. It was in that moment, as I gazed again out my window, that God clearly spoke to me.

His voice was like nothing I had heard before! It was not like thunder or lightning, but rather it was still and clear, just as Elijah had described it. The way God spoke to me then, and the way he continues to speak to me now, is through an interruption in my mind and thoughts. In the midst of a thought process or even during a conversation with someone, he just interrupts my thinking. His voice is strong, clear and undeniably God.

Right there, in the back seat of our family's Ford, God said, *"This is the girl you are going to marry, the girl you have always prayed for."*

An electric current ran through me as my head jolted from the window to Mary, and then back again to the window. "No way." I thought. "God finally speaks to me...and he says this? I must be losing my mind."

It's hard to describe exactly what happened to my heart in the moments that followed. All I can tell you is that when I turned my head to once again look at Mary, I fell helplessly and deeply in love with her. Everything about her suddenly seemed to be so incredibly perfect and beautiful. I distinctly remember the absurdity of looking at the fine hairs on her arm and thinking that even in something as simple as that, I saw her unbelievable beauty.

I was like a man struck dumb. God knew my heart, and in my heart of hearts I had longed for a good woman to be my wife and a mother to my children. In the midst of searching for God, Mary suddenly became a vital piece of the puzzle. I was filled with an electrifying feeling that couldn't be contained. This supernatural experience of divine revelation had caused me to become a blubbering idiot for the rest of the evening. My quick-spoken, jumbled words not only confused Mary, but they also confused everyone else at our banquet table.

I could tell that my family and friends noticed something was off about me, but I just couldn't get a hold of myself. Bud pulled me aside asking, "What's wrong with you, Charles?" Of course my mother also noticed and asked if I was okay. But I was better than okay. I had heard the voice of the Lord! Finally, he had spoken, revealing his voice to me. At last I knew it was really God, and he was bringing about his promises in my life. Now if only he could tell that to Mary.

I was seated right next to Mary's father at the banquet table, and perhaps I made a fool of myself when I turned to him after one short car ride with his daughter and said, "Mr. Lou, I am going to marry your daughter."

He laughed amusedly, saying, "As long as you have a good job, Chief." I caught Mary's eyes as she glared at me interrogatively and asked, "What's your game?"

How could I possibly explain it to her? How could I tell her that when Bud and I picked her and Pauline up earlier that evening, I didn't care for her at all. I only asked her on the date in the first place to satisfy my mom and grandpop. She was just supposed to be a casual date for the banquet.

And yet, my life changed forever on that car ride. God had finally spoken to me, and of all the things he could have said, he told me that I would marry her, Mary Longo!

Well, you can imagine how quickly it became clear to me that I couldn't just share God's revelation with Mary and expect her to go pick out her wedding dress. No, God expected much more of me than that. I would have to *win* Mary's heart and convince her to be mine.

I asked God *why* he had revealed this to me. The answer was because he loved me, and because I had been unceasingly searching for him since I was a young boy. My quest for him was a hunger–a breath I wanted more than a drowning man.

God heard me knocking throughout the years, and he in turn gave me this gift–the gift of hearing his voice. And hearing his voice that first time became a very special landmark in my life, because it was just the beginning of my long journey with him. I slowly was discovering his will for me, and he was allowing me to see his handiwork in it. God still wanted me to fulfill the call of my heart, which in this case was fighting valiantly to win Mary's.

Hearing God's voice and his answer to my youthful prayer was a cornerstone in my walk with him. He gave me an actual *experience* of faith, one that I have never forgotten. Thankfully, the Lord also gave me the true desires of my heart, realized in Mary.

Over the next several years, Mary discovered just how true my intentions were, and she in turn fell deeper in love with me. During our relationship, I walked away from all ties to my showbiz career, as well as my short stint in the Navy. I finally realized that someone truly loved me for who I was.

The fulfillment of this desire was deeper and more satisfying than I had ever thought possible, and greatly exceeded my every expectation. God had been preparing me for her, and she for me, and our union was more than I could ever have imagined.

> *"Ask, and it will be given you; seek, and you will find; knock, and it will be opened to you." (Matthew 7:7)*

I was seeking, I was knocking, and he gave me the companion who would bring many others and me closer to him.

I fought for her and finally won her heart. When Mary was nineteen and I was twenty-one, we were married and became one flesh in Christ. I wrote her this poem:

> *"Of all the things that God has made,*
> *Not one of them could be,*
> *Possessed more with the things I love,*
> *Then whom He gave to me."*

You would have expected that after attaining such a pearl of great price and hearing the Lord speak to me that I would be forever on the path toward righteousness. But man is plagued with sin. Although Mary faithfully attended Mass every Sunday, it was not something I was willing to do just yet.

Shortly after our marriage, I allowed confusion to again cloud my vision and redirect my path. I was still trying to walk down two conflicting roads at the same time. I had one foot firmly on the way of the Lord, and one foot stuck on the way of the world, and it wasn't long before I slipped right back into my selfish desires.

"Woe to timid hearts and to slack hands, and to the sinner who walks along two ways!" (Sirach 2:12)

Still yearning to fill my sense of importance, I thought I could achieve my own desires without the Lord. I was so naïve that I didn't realize how much I needed him for everything, and that God was calling me to surrender my own will and decrease myself, so that he could increase his will within me.

My great struggle was how to let go of my need for personal pride. I knew I needed to rid myself of the desire to be commended by others. In fact, the life that Christ was preparing me for would be quite the opposite. He offered me no power, but rather he invited me to accept and trust in his.

Through baby steps he began to prepare me for the great spiritual gifts he would soon entrust to me.

CHAPTER THREE

A Baby and a Breast Tumor

Mary and I loved the same thing–she loved me, and I loved me! But Mary also loved God and her Catholic faith. That presented a problem for us, as I had sworn off the Church and all institutional religious practices.

Naturally, I tried to get Mary on board with my disordered spiritual beliefs. Maybe if I could convince her to accept my philosophy, I wouldn't have to address religion per se. In the meantime, I refused to take part in her Catholic practices, and I criticized them as often as I could.

Intellectually, I felt I couldn't reduce God to being present in any one particular organized religion. The truth was that the mysteries of God certainly could not be contained in the mind of man. I just couldn't see it then.

Regardless of how deeply I loved Mary, there was no way I could take serious the superstitious Catholic "mumbo jumbo" she clung to. But to her credit, she never strayed from her faithfulness to the teachings of Catholicism despite my doubts.

Mary also didn't see me as I saw me–the bold sojourner carving out my own path toward God. Rather, Mary became more and more frightened of me and insecure in her decision to have married me. She began thinking, "What have I done, Lord? Who is this man?"

As I would later discover, Mary drove to Mass alone on one of those first Sundays after we were married, and she sat in the church parking lot crying desperately in her car. It was really through her strength and faithfulness that God was able to pull me back on board.

We soon moved into our first small apartment on the second floor of a row house in Baltimore. I remember fondly the first two evening meals Mary made for me there. They were really a comedy! Our kitchen was so small that only two people could fit in it comfortably at a time. I can't imagine how she managed to make anything in that space.

Knowing how much I loved spaghetti with meatballs and sausage, she planned the perfect surprise for me. Arriving home from work, the smell of sauce lured me up the two flights of stairs to our apartment. "Have a seat, Honey," Mary said happily as I entered. She was already in the process of fixing me a plate, and my stomach could hardly stand the wait.

I tried not to let the shock on my face show, as a plate of wet noodles with tomato skins was set before me. The watered down concoction was piled high and crowned with a small sausage on top. I had never seen anything like this before.

Mary sat down before her plate, which looked similar to mine— but instead of a sausage, hers had a small meatball on top. All I could think was, "Good thing Grandma isn't here to see this!"

I smiled at her as I picked up my fork, and we began to eat. After a few moments of silence, Mary stopped and said, "Honey, I don't think this has any taste." Boy was she right! Knowing how important it was to her though, I smiled and said, "It's fine, Honey. I'll just have another sausage or meatball." She looked back at me with sadness in her eyes and said, "There are no more. I only have one of each."

In response to my puzzled expression, she went on to explain that she had confidently asked the butcher to give her a quarter pound of sausage and a quarter pound of ground beef. She didn't realize how little a quarter pound of meat was, until she got home. I can't tell you how hysterical my friends at work were the next day when I told them about my first meal in our new home. It's things like that that stick with you–the joys of our journey together in marriage.

I can't say the meals got better anytime soon. In fact, I found myself cautiously scaling the stairs the next day after work, half expecting the place to be on fire. As I got closer and closer to our apartment door, my eyes began to water. "Have I got a surprise for you," Mary said as I came through the door. She ushered me toward the table, and I hesitantly sat down as she placed a plate of dark, dry beef before me, followed by a large pot of gravy, and charred muffins. Again, she seemed very pleased with herself as she said, "You won't go hungry tonight, dear!"

I had to admit that the tanned muffins on the top of the gravy in the pot reminded me of the delicious crust of my mother's home-cooked pie. However, when I attempted to dip the large serving spoon into the gravy, it dropped to the bottom of the pot with a loud clink. Everything under the muffins had burned away. We found ourselves laughing over dry beef and burnt muffins, and I had yet another story to take back to the guys at work.

We can laugh about it now, mostly because Mary has become an excellent cook. Those were just some of the early growing pains of marriage. Our time together in that apartment was very memorable, but challenges were about to come.

About a year after living in the apartment, much to our great joy, Mary became pregnant. Each night I would listen and place my hand on her belly, hoping to hear or feel our child. It was a magical time. Three months into the pregnancy, however, she noticed a large lump on one of her breasts. We both hoped it was nothing to be concerned about, but we decided to address it with her doctor.

After giving Mary a thorough examination, her doctor, who was also a surgeon, gave us a frightening prognosis. Mary had a suspicious tumor on her breast that he wanted to remove immediately. We both went numb as he continued talking, wondering if we were facing cancer, and if so, how it would affect our lives and the baby's.

One thing was certain–he didn't want to waste any time. Mary's doctor explained to us that the tumor needed to be removed and biopsied immediately. There was a great risk, because if the tumor was cancerous, there was a potential for the cancer to spread throughout Mary's body. The next thing we knew, the appointment was set for surgery, and we were on our way to Mercy Medical Center. We both were scared.

We arrived at the hospital the night before the procedure. It was admittedly difficult for both of us to get through that restless night. In the morning, a nurse came into the room and gave Mary a mild sedative to help calm her before surgery. My mother-in-law arrived at the hospital, and she and I sat quietly with Mary, who began drifting off to sleep.

I found myself helpless and paralyzed with fear. The only thing I knew to do in that moment was to bow my head and internally ask the Lord to hear my prayer. "Lord, I know you can do anything you want at any time," I cried out to him. "I know you can take this tumor away right now," I implored. "I don't want her to suffer with this. Please take it away, Lord." He had spoken to me once before, and I knew he could easily do so again. So why not now? I needed him to speak to me now. But there was no response.

My mother-in-law and I sat quietly beside Mary's gurney, waiting until the nurses came to wheel her away. I could hear every muffled sound and movement from the silence of that hospital room—nurses talking, someone's shoes on the linoleum hallway floor—and then I heard God's voice.

He spoke to me so clearly that I was sure it had been audible. I turned to my mother-in-law and asked if she had heard it. She looked at me confused. "No, I didn't hear anything," she responded. "Why, what did you hear?" she asked.

I paused for a moment, and then just said it. "I heard God speak to me."

It was a bold proclamation, and to her credit, she gently asked, "What did he say?"

Finding my voice, I responded, "He said, 'okay, it's gone.'"

She looked at me utterly perplexed and asked, "What's gone?"

With a combination of panic and joy, I proclaimed, "Mary's tumor!"

She glanced down at the ground for a moment and then looked me in the eyes and began calmly reassuring me. Putting her hand on mine, she said, "They'll be taking her down soon, and I'm sure they'll check before they operate."

I knew it must have been hard for her to fathom what I had just said, much less begin to know what to do with it. Clearly she thought I was speaking out of fear and grasping at straws of hope. I knew, however, that was not the case. I had to do something! I had to act on what God had just told me.

Leaning over Mary's gurney, I tried to wake her. "See if the lump is still there," I whispered down to her.

In her groggy state of sedation, she felt under her gown, and sleepily answered, "Yes, I think so." Hmm, the physical evidence still seemed to not be there, but I had to trust God's word despite this.

Regardless of the worried expression on my mother-in-law's face as Mary continued feeling for the lump–and the trouble my news surely would cause the doctor and nurses–I knew in my heart I couldn't let them take Mary to surgery. I had every faith that the voice I heard was that of the Lord, and I needed to act upon it. He was again asking me to believe what he said to me, despite the odds. God truly was testing my faith.

When the nurses at last came in to wheel Mary down to the operating room, I knew it was my moment to stand with the Lord, regardless of how foolish I might appear to everyone at the hospital. Collecting my courage, I firmly said to them, "I can't let you take her down."

With a look of understanding concern, the nurses began to assure me of Mary's safety. Stoically I continued, "I don't think you understand, I am sure her tumor is gone, and I want the doctor to come up here and check her."

The nurses glanced back and forth at one another, not quite sure how to respond. One of them finally said, "But Mr. Piccirilli, the doctor is prepped for surgery." Seeing that I would not be persuaded, she tried again saying, "We will make sure he checks her again when she goes down."

I still could not allow it. Swallowing the lump in my throat, I remained firm answering, "No, he has to come up here."

Although my mother-in-law was becoming visibly upset, she remained silent. The nurses left the room in a hurry, returning minutes later with the doctor. I remember well the look of annoyance on his face as he stood in the doorway, dressed in scrubs and blue medical booties. "What's going on?" he demanded.

Taking a step toward him, I said, "I believe my wife's tumor is gone, and I want you to check her now." He looked at me with astonishment and then quizzically at the nurses. After a few moments, he angrily told Mary's mother and me to leave the room. We walked out quickly and stood in the hallway for ten agonizing minutes, just waiting.

I'm sure in those moments my mother-in-law thought I was painfully prolonging the inevitable. The medical staff certainly thought I was nuts, but I gave that moment to the Lord.

Finally, the doctor broke our silent anticipation by flinging open the door and stepping out into the hallway. He looked squarely at me and said, "Go home. It's gone." With that, he marched down the hallway in a stupor, shaking his head as he walked away.

"Oh my Jesus, thank you so much, I knew you could do it. What a good and glorious God of might you are," my praises rang out. Mary's mother and I went back into the room and helped Mary dress and collect her things as the sedative wore off. Together, the three of us left the hospital on angel's wings, and we went to a small restaurant across the street to celebrate over breakfast.

FOUR

What's Wrong with Rose & Bob?

After the incredible miracle of the instant healing of Mary's breast tumor, we once again returned to our happy life in our cozy apartment. Our focus now was solely on the dawning of our new parenthood. For seven glorious months we reveled in the joy of this expectation. We read, prepared, decorated, and most importantly, shared our joyous anticipation with family members.

With only two months to go, Mary began to experience difficulties. One night this escalated to the point of profuse bleeding. As I carefully helped her into the car and raced to the hospital, we once again found ourselves facing a great fear. But this time it ended differently.

Our happy dream came to an end. Mary's hospital gown was soaked with tears as she told me the news that we had lost our baby. A dagger pierced my heart at that moment. There was nothing more that could be done–no prayer, and no answer. Sadly, we left the hospital alone and headed home.

In those days we didn't know if our baby was a boy or girl, but both having the strong inclination that he had been a boy, we gave our child the name Adam.

The grief of the miscarriage left me very distraught. Why would God allow this to happen to me? Having very little theological formation, I wondered if Adam's life had simply ceased to exist altogether. Perhaps his energy was hovering around us, or his soul was waiting to be reincarnated.

Shortly after the miscarriage, my father and I sat around talking. I told him that I believed Adam was waiting to be reborn as our second child, which seemed legitimate enough to the both of us.

Eighteen months passed, with the grief of the miscarriage finally beginning to settle, and Mary again became pregnant. We were both hopeful and ready to once again experience the great joy of expectation a pregnancy brings.

This second pregnancy showed us God working another wonder in our lives, and it gave us renewed hope. I was sure it would be a boy, and I planned to name him Micah, after the sheriff on the television series The Rifleman. Mary agreed, because Micah was also a biblical name.

Mary's pregnancy was wonderful this time, with relatively no complications or alarms. And after those nine months, Mary made me a father by giving me a son. Micah was born safe and sound.

God used that moment of Micah's birth in a powerful way. My whole attitude began to change, just as I'm sure it does for many fathers when they experience the birth of their first child.

Suddenly I was a father, and this small miracle depended on me. I felt incredibly strong and undeniably scared at the same time. It was as if the dawning of a new life was beginning for Charles Piccirilli in that moment. I had a new reason to exist.

Micah's birth not only fueled my motivation to work even harder to support my family, but it also was the catalyst that finally began to turn me away from my selfishness.

I started my own graphic design business, and I was filled with visions of wonderful success. That success was very slow to come though, and we lived paycheck to paycheck, if we were lucky.

The stress of the business and trying to make ends meet consumed me, filling me with worry and anxiety. My family began to see less and less of me, as I disappeared into my work for long hours that turned into nights and weekends.

As I continued to hack it out on my own, the exhaustion and hopelessness almost swallowed me alive. "Why couldn't I succeed in making this business work?" I thought agonizingly. "How could I be working so hard and getting deeper and deeper into debt?" I was angry and going nowhere. Again, I needed a savior.

Then one evening, as I frantically looked over my checkbook, my heart began to sink. Realizing I was further in debt than I had thought, I finally surrendered the pride that had been driving me to do this on my own. Fortunately for me, God was preparing the next step of my journey toward his love, through my accountant brother-in-law.

Mary's sister Rose had married a stable man named Bob, who took over my accounting. Mary and I both liked Bob and enjoyed spending time with him and Rose. True to his German nature, my accountant brother-in-law was more comfortable with numbers than outward affection. You can imagine how uncomfortable it was for him to be part of our demonstrative Italian family!

It was certainly unnatural to Bob when we kissed each and every family member, whether we were coming or going. Bob would tense up like a board whenever this awkward exchange took place. He was much happier to just slip out unnoticed than to participate.

Bob was a generous man though, and he would help me with the books and taxes for my business anytime I needed him… and this time I really needed him. So when he and Rose stopped by, I was especially happy. Mary and Rose went into the kitchen while Bob and I sat opposite each other at the dining room table. As we wandered off the financial topic from time to time, he began to share a bit about a meeting he had attended. I didn't know it then, but this would be the next piece in God's puzzle for me.

"I was touched, Charles, truly touched by God," he said in amazement as he described the meeting. Now I was the one who felt awkward. To openly share something so personal was very unusual for Bob...and about God? What in the world was he talking about? Were he and Rose going to some kind of a church group, I wondered? This time I was the one who quickly turned our attention back to the numbers.

Mary and Rose eventually let us know that it was getting late, and Bob and I wrapped things up for the night. As he and Rose walked toward the door, Mary and I stood there ready to say good night. Then Bob did something that made all of our jaws drop. Mary, Rose, and I went through our usual greeting and departure ritual, intentionally leaving Bob out. But he joined right in this time, hugging and kissing Mary. Then turning toward me, he reached out and genuinely cupped my hands in his!

Mary and I just stared at each other when the door finally closed. We couldn't wash the surprise off our faces. Our wide eyes and big smiles seemed to say it all, "Wow, what in the world happened to him?" Whatever it was, it had to be something truly extraordinary to change a stiff man like Bob into the heartwarming character we had just encountered.

But Bob wasn't the only one affected by this meeting. We soon discovered that the same transformation had happened in Rose as well. Somehow, both of them seemingly were changed overnight. Of course my curiosity and skepticism got the better of me, as I continued to ponder this metamorphosis. I determined that I needed to know more.

I wanted to go to this meeting, but it was by no means for the purpose of seeking transformation. No, I wanted to see what they were selling. This thing reeked of institutional religion, and I was ready for a fight.

The funny thing is, I had no proper formation, plus a severe lack of scriptural knowledge, and was wavering in the wind on the principles of my own faith beliefs. Yet, despite all this, I somehow believed that no one could prove me wrong. I was in serious need of direction and a good dose of humility. Pride goes before destruction, and I was about to be demolished by Christ.

The non-denominational gathering of Christians went by the name of *New Life*, and it met for weekly prayer meetings in the basement of a Catholic school. It all seemed very cliché to me, as Mary and I were greeted by smiles all around. I tried not to let their warm and welcoming attention get in the way of my mission to set these people straight.

Mary and I were led into a small side room with a few other new people, before joining the regulars in the main area. Here we were presented with a formal introduction to the prayer meeting. I let most of that information go in one ear and out the other, as I had come loaded with my own questions ready to pelt at them. I was sure that once I had blown the lid off this thing, Mary and I would be out the door before it even got off the ground. Hopefully, we would be bringing Bob and Rose with us.

I couldn't help but begin to tune in, however, as the man leading the introduction started answering my questions one by one. The only problem was that I hadn't *asked* them yet. Something was certainly afoot. He couldn't actually have encountered all of these questions before.

I felt the sweat on my forehead begin to bead up. Were these people clairvoyants? I had met many people trying to achieve clairvoyance in my past, but none like this. My skepticism and intrigue were at odds within me, and I was completely enthralled.

I sat quietly, now realizing the necessity of a slyer approach and perhaps a new strategy. As we joined the others in the main room, the meeting began, and oh boy did it begin!

People were singing and praying out loud. They carried on, even dancing and crying out their unprompted praise to God. There was scripture reading and bouts of random gibberish. It was unsettling and overwhelming to say the least. I looked at my wife, and she looked at me. "We've got to get out of here," I whispered loudly to Mary. "The men are hugging each other!"

Mary looked just as jarred, but as usual, she took the prudent approach saying, "Let's wait and see what happens." She didn't want to be rude, and I'm thankful now that we stayed. As the people around us continued standing in front of their chairs shouting, "Praise God, Praise God," I noticed a little boy in the mix.

He was happily woven in the crowd of adults, praising with a genuine innocence and joy that convinced me he really did believe what was happening. He didn't seem brainwashed, as I would have imagined. Rather, he seemed like he was right at home. In fact, it seemed that he was in his child-like comfort zone, and it was the adults who were stepping out in faith. They were allowing themselves to be vulnerable and foolish. And in doing so, they were free, fully free, to praise God uninhibitedly.

Because of that little boy's faith example, I bowed my head and said, "God if you are really here, come into my life."

Now I will give a word to the wise here. When you invite the Holy Spirit into your life, expect extraordinary things to happen! As I sat there, my chair suddenly began to shake violently. I turned to Mary and asked, "Is your chair shaking?"

She looked at me oddly saying, "No."

With a look of panic, I then turned to Bob, who was sitting on the other side of me. "Is your chair shaking, Bob?" I asked him.

He also looked at me with concern saying, "No."

I stared straight ahead, suddenly feeling very isolated in that crowded room. How was it that the chairs to my right and left were not shaking, and yet mine was vibrating so badly that I had to hold on so as not to fall off? Didn't any of these people notice that my chair was shaking all over the place?

And then it hit me. I realized that the tremendous shaking was not coming from the chairs. It was coming from inside of me. Something powerful was happening–something I couldn't deny. There was a raging battle taking place within me, and I knew it was for control of my soul.

At that first prayer meeting Mary and I attended, I unquestionably encountered the Holy Spirit. It was the first of many prayer meetings to follow. In fact, we eventually even entered a covenant of devoted discipline to the *New Life* community, which ultimately aided my return to the Catholic Church, as well as fostering a deep relationship with Jesus Christ.

I had always been a disciplined man, but I was sorely and gravely lacking in spiritual discipline. I already had the discipline to work long hours, meet deadlines, and present myself well in the business world, but my spiritual path was like jello–you couldn't pin me to anything.

After so many weary years of giving my life to many forms of the occult, there was no room within me for the Holy Spirit. If I was now truly asking the Holy Spirit to come, then somebody else had to go.

This was a spiritual surgery I had not anticipated. How could I have known there wouldn't be room within me for both the Holy Spirit and the darkness of the occult? But it became all too clear that the many evil spirits I had invited to enter my soul over the years had to go, and they didn't go willingly.

I actually had to kick them out. I had to surrender my dark pursuits of reading the future, becoming a medium, and all other disordered forms of obtaining spiritual power. God needed me to be his fully, and he was asking for permission to clean house.

It was then, at our first prayer meeting, that I said "yes," to God. I was ready to be rid of the demons once and for all. It was a very frightening experience, however, as the spirits left in a violent and angry way. Previously, I had seen and communicated with dark figures around me quite often. But it was when I actually cried out the name of "Jesus," that they became threatening. I heard audible, nasty threats as they left.

And then they were gone, never to return.

The Lord taught me a lesson that day that I will never forget. My soul was in serious jeopardy, and he needed to show me the dangerous reality of hell. The familiar spirits who darkened my mind and soul wanted nothing more than my spiritual demise.

Frightened out of my mind that night, I vowed to never again even attempt to make contact with them. Because of my ability to sense evil spirits a mile away, the Lord has since used me as a threat to them henceforth. Many times, I have called upon the Lord for the sake of myself and others, who were under similar attacks by the same consuming darkness.

> *"Every kingdom divided against itself is laid waste,*
> *and no city or house divided against itself will stand...*
> *But if it is by the Spirit of God that I cast out demons,*
> *then the kingdom of God has come upon you."*
> *(Matthew 12:25, 28)*

Mary and I were not the same two people when we left the prayer meeting that evening. And we didn't leave alone either. From that point on, the Holy Spirit and the kingdom of God were with us both!

FIVE

Take Away my Four Packs a Day

Could God heal me of a physical addiction when all else had failed? The morning after that first prayer meeting, I believed he could. I knew that God was very near, and so I laid my first fleece before him, like Gideon had in Judges 6:37. Perhaps it seemed trivial and unimportant, but smoking had become real bondage, and I was aching to be free. I promised the Lord I would never smoke again, if only he would help me quit.

I was just nine years old when I started smoking. That may shock you, but addiction was all part of the lifestyle I began gravitating toward at an early age. As I conveyed earlier, my soul was very much a house divided against itself.

My dad had been a big smoker, and the only person who smoked more than him was grandpop. Seeing how thoroughly they both enjoyed it, I knew I needed to give it a try. I snuck into grandpop's room, and having grabbed one of his cigarettes, I ran and hid away with it at our family's construction site, which was only a stone's throw away.

Beyond the initial bad taste, there was actually quite an exhilaration that came along with it. After all, I was getting away with something I knew I shouldn't be doing, and I liked it. This early experience of illicit satisfaction gave me my first taste of the evil desire for sin lurking within.

I also remember vividly the first time my father caught me smoking. Somehow he found a pack of cigarettes in my room. At first he tried to conceal his disgust, but it was evident that he intended to put a stop to it immediately. He grabbed the pack of cigarettes and instructed me to follow him outside. "So you want to smoke?" he asked handing me a cigarette. "Okay, let's do it together," he said as he lit one up.

I hesitantly started to puff on the cigarette, and we smoked side by side in silence. When I finally finished and snuffed out the butt, he was right there to light another for me. This continued in hopes that I would become so sick from smoking the whole pack that I would never think of another cigarette again. Yet, when we at last reached the end of the pack and I continued to stand by stoically, he disgustedly told me to go to bed as he walked off in frustration and defeat.

Looking back, it's hard to remember any part of my past without a cigarette. Smoking was just part of who I was. Of course, I never considered the struggle of addiction or the health consequences that would later come with it. But as the years went on and I climbed up to two packs a day, my lungs began to resent me. I developed breathing troubles that became so intense I couldn't even play sports as a teen. I finally became convinced that I was killing, or at least crippling, myself. That was the first time I made an honest attempt to quit.

It was also the first time I truly understood the spirit's will against the flesh's weakness! I became extremely aggravated when I discovered that I couldn't exert my will power enough to stop the addiction. I laugh now, remembering myself as a prideful teenage boy, trying to quit. Working for the family construction business, I had great confidence that I was a tough guy and could rule my own desires. So when my desire for a cigarette began eating me alive, I did everything I could to hide it from the other workers.

One day as we were on the job site, after announcing that I had quit smoking, I could think of nothing else. When my father wasn't looking, I grabbed whatever I could find to satisfy my need for a smoke. Reduced to desperation, I wound up rolling some straw in a paper cement bag and tried to smoke that. I even went so far as to try lettuce cigarettes, which were arguably even worse than the cement bag.

After those brutal failed attempts, I just gave in to the addiction. I continued smoking more and more, until I finally reached a whopping four packs a day. The next day after our first prayer meeting, at the age of thirty-one, as I stared down at the cigarette pack in front of me, I became painfully aware that I could never quit on my own.

Knowing the power that this addiction had over me physically, and the newfound power of the Holy Spirit now within me, I decided to call upon the Lord for freedom. My prayer sounded something like this, "Lord, I am going to finish this pack of cigarettes, and then I promise you, I will never smoke again. But you know I can't do it without your help. Amen."

Looking to savor that last and final pack of Marlboros, I grabbed a cigarette, put it in my mouth, and pressed the flame to it. As much as I wanted to enjoy that last pack of smokes, I could not. My face cringed at the smell. How could I have not noticed how repulsive the smell was before? As I stubbed out the cigarette in the ashtray, disgusted by the stale taste it left in my mouth, I suddenly realized that God had taken away my desire completely. From that moment, the desire to smoke was gone, and I threw away the remaining pack. More than forty years later, I have never smoked again.

Perhaps this instantaneous healing seems insignificant to anyone who never has been bound by such an addiction–but to those of us who have, the magnitude of this kind of freedom is colossal! After this deliverance, I felt the grace to help others who also were struggling and bound by addiction. Through the years, God allowed me to see many freed in the same way I had been.

Mary and I had been attending the New Life prayer meetings faithfully on Friday nights. One evening, as we made our way down the basement stairs of St. Margaret's Catholic School, I realized that somewhere along the way we had become those welcoming and joyful people, the same ones I had criticized the first time we came. We not only were coming regularly, but we also had decided to take the next step in becoming part of the committed core group.

Together, we were growing in deep holiness, seeking the Lord, immersing ourselves in scripture and prayer, and learning to ask for forgiveness. We grew in love for each other as well. Through our faults and imperfections, we were learning to love each other as the Lord intended, in him and through him.

There also were many other new people attending the meetings as word of the strong community prayer life spread, and of course there were always those attending out of curiosity. One evening, George and Bernice attended for the first time. George was an elderly gentleman and a heavy smoker. He always wore a shirt with a breast pocket that protruded from his chest, boasting the box of cigarettes stuffed within.

His many years of smoking certainly had taken its toll on his health. When I asked him how much he smoked a day, George answered begrudgingly, "Three packs." When I asked him if he wanted to quit, he answered me as most smokers do, both enthusiastically and fearfully. "Yes, of course I do," he snapped. Having only recently suffered from the same addiction myself, I shared my healing story with George.

He was certainly curious to hear more, although he seemed convinced that it would be far more impossible for him to break free of his own addiction. Still I went on, explaining how there was no way I could have done it on my own. I painted the picture for him of my sitting with my last pack of cigarettes before me, promising God I would never smoke again if he would only remove the desire from me. George listened intently as I spoke of repentance and desire.

I often like to use analogous stories to get my point across, so I said to George, "This reminds me of the story about a man walking a tightrope over a canyon while pushing a wheelbarrow." George just looked at me, trying to figure out where the story was going. "The tightrope walker looked back at the spectators and called out to them, 'Do you believe now that I can do this?'" I paused before continuing, "One spectator shouted his 'yes' to the tightrope walker, who glanced at his wheelbarrow and said, "Then get in!'"

We both laughed for a minute, but George got the point. "You have to 'get in', George," I said seriously. "Toss the cigarettes. Promise the Lord you will never smoke again. Just ask for his help and his grace to follow through." George looked at me with new hope creeping into his eyes, and I knew that my testimony about God's miraculous power had instilled in him a new measure of faith.

Sure enough, the following week George waltzed right through the doors of the prayer meeting with a big smile on his face. Making a beeline for me, he tapped his empty shirt pocket. "Look, Charlie," he said. "No more cigarettes! I did what you said, and God took my addiction away. I will never smoke again."

I was very happy for George—not only because he was free from his addiction, but also because his faith continued to grow bolder and stronger as a result of this experience with the Lord. He bounced confidently into the meetings for the next several weeks.

But then one Friday, George came in slowly, dragging one leg behind the other. His face was twisted in a painful grimace.

"George, what's wrong?" I asked as he lowered himself into a seat.

In a voice that was full of grimace, he softly answered, "As I was cutting the grass, my lawnmower blade broke off and hit me in the leg." My face contorted at the thought of what he'd experienced.

"Let me see," I said bracing myself. George lifted his pant leg to reveal a red and swollen lump on his shin about the size of half a baseball. It appeared to be a nasty and painful protrusion.

The meeting began, but I couldn't help thinking about George. When it came time to pray for those in need, I looked over at him, and he raised his hand to volunteer himself. As we gathered around him to pray, I knelt by his leg, getting as close as I could. He lifted his pant leg, and I cupped my hand over the very warm and hard lump. Then we all began to pray, asking God's healing for George's leg. As I knelt there beside him and heard the showering of prayers from the others around us, I suddenly felt the lump disappear right under my hand!

It happened so fast, in less than a minute's time. Just a moment before, my whole hand had been filled with the swollen mass from his shin, and now it was flat and cool to the touch. I pulled my hand back quickly to confirm with my own eyes. There was no sign of the lump. It was truly gone in an instant!

I looked up at George, and I could tell by the speechless surprise on his face that he was equally aware of the healing that had taken place. We were both frozen for a moment, eyes as big as silver dollars, and stunned by what just happened. "Did you feel that?" I asked George as he repeated the same question to me, "Did you feel it too?" Then, as if on cue, we both began to acknowledge the miracle and listened to the chorus of prayer all around us.

The funny thing is, that because none of the others knew what George and I knew about the healing, they were still asking the Lord for a miracle. While George and I were both praising the Lord for the miracle that had just taken place. When it finally became apparent to those around us that their prayers and our thanksgiving were not in unison, they stopped. George and I excitedly showed them that the lump was gone, and George was healed. Laughter and joy broke out and moved through us like a crashing wave, and we began jumping and shouting praise and thanksgiving like children.

I looked down at my own hand in a strange sort of amazement. Moments earlier, it had wrapped around the lump on George's leg. That's all it did. The Lord did the rest. "Wow, Lord." I thought amazedly. "You can use anyone's hands, if only we will extend them in prayer, trusting your gift of faith."

SIX

If You're Really Here, Say This

Part of my powerful conversion occurred through the formal joining of the *New Life* prayer group with Mary. We had been serving and attending as core group leaders for a while now, and all of us felt called to something more—a covenant. In the end, Rose and Bob had given us an extraordinary gift when they had invited us to that first prayer meeting, one that has enriched our ongoing journey with the Lord.

In its foundational stages, the leadership of New Life decided we were being called to become a covenant community. This meant far more than just meeting in the basement of St. Margaret's School once a week. Now we would have accountability to one another, making it our duty to help get our brothers and sisters in community to heaven. No more shying away from heavy topics or turning our eyes from the troubles of our brothers. Their troubles were now our troubles. The meetings would forever remain open to anyone wanting to join us in prayer, but for those who felt called to a personal commitment, it was so much more.

As the Holy Spirit continued his work in me, I knew the Lord wanted me to plant my feet somewhere solid. It was time for this "jello" to firm up. Knowing that I needed to be under spiritual authority, I also felt called to join a lay movement. The Lord was asking me to surrender my "yes" to him. I didn't need to bounce all over to find him. He was asking me to say to him, "I will be right here Lord, in good times and bad. I will trust that you will find me here, and bless me right here."

I was pulling up a chair at the banquet table he provided, and it was at that table I remained, regardless of what was served. At times, we metaphorically feasted on steak as kings, and at other times we were lucky to have a piece of bread.

Our covenant held us accountable to showing up at prayer meetings, and committing to the investment of a physical location for our community and the needs of that space. It also held us accountable to respecting leadership. We chose the humblest men to lead the group in all the circumstances God would provide along the way. We discerned and prayed with one another, ultimately holding each other accountable to Christ.

Because we never compromised our various Christian beliefs, we remained focused on what we had in common—namely Christ, scripture, the virtues, the beatitudes, the commandments, and the Christian community. But the overwhelming number of Catholics in that group eventually provided another strong influence on me.

One incident occurred in the early days of our prayer meetings, and it concerned a woman named Jan. Mary and I had been friends with Jan and her husband Lou even before our encounter with Christ. In our younger and wilder days, we would get together regularly with them and a few other couples to enjoy fun parties at their house.

As Mary and I continued to grow more in love with the Lord and become more excited about our prayer meetings, we naturally wanted to share what we had with Jan and Lou. I was on fire with zeal and gushed about how wild horses couldn't drag me away from that special time to praise the Lord each week. And whenever we began speaking like this in front of Jan and Lou, they became even more guarded and skeptical than we had ever been. But of course, out of curiosity, they had to see for themselves.

When Jan and Lou came to that first prayer meeting, they reminded me quite a bit of myself the first time I had come.

They were sitting stiffly in the back row, and I can only image what they must have been thinking as I took out my guitar and began singing with the music ministry. When it came time for quiet prayer, Jan and Lou looked around at everyone. Some of us sat with hands folded and heads down, while others joyfully read through their bibles–but all with hearts open, ready to be moved.

In my own silence, I heard the voice of God. It wasn't audible, and yet clearly not my own thought. These interruptions had become more and more familiar to me. I was not able to force them, and they often made no immediate sense. This time, the Lord said something very quietly and simply, *"Say, 'I am your shepherd; you shall not want.'"*

Upon hearing this, I immediately glanced around the room of people in quiet prayer. I fidgeted for a few moments, uncomfortable with what the Lord had asked me to say. I began reasoning with myself, "Everyone here has a bible, and I'm sure they understand the psalm better than me." But then again, as true as this may have been, the Lord had asked me to speak. Perhaps the thing that bothered me the most about this request was how presumptuous it might sound, repeating the psalm from a first-person perspective. I asked the Lord, "Shouldn't I say, 'The Lord is my shepherd; I shall not want?'"

So instead of piping up as instructed, I sat and pondered the depth of the scripture, considering what it might mean to the people around me. I couldn't imagine just blurting out, "The Lord wants me to say, 'I am your shepherd; you shall not want.'"

Wouldn't I feel like a fool without any clear explanation to offer? I began to think fast. "Maybe God wants us to know that we should not be greedy for things," I thought. "Or perhaps he is reminding us that he really is our supplier, and the source of all our needs."

I wrestled with my dilemma, trying to rally the courage to deliver the words I knew God had given me to say. After thinking about it for most of the meeting, squirming in my chair, I finally decided to stand up and speak. I figured, "Oh well, what have I got to lose? I will just say it, and then add my own interpretation at the end as an added bonus!"

But just as I was about to speak, the Lord interrupted me again. "No. Just say: 'I am your shepherd; you shall not want." That made it clear and final. He didn't want my exegesis. He was doing something else. So with that, I stood up and proclaimed, "I am your shepherd; you shall not want."

I sat back down just as quickly as I had stood up. A wave of tremendous guilt and embarrassment washed over me. "Who do I think I am?" I thought. "I'm not God. I'm not some mystical or holy person. Who am I to speak these words and assume that they are coming from God?" The evil one was certainly giving me a pummeling. "Do I really think that God would speak his words through me?"

Unfortunately, this tremendous self-condemnation is still quite common after sharing words spoken by the Lord. I always feel certain that I'll never open my mouth again. But the man sitting on my left nudged me, jolting me out of my censure. "You're about to see a miracle," he said.

"Really?" I asked. How do you know?" Perhaps he thought it was what I needed to hear after seeing how embarrassed I appeared to be.

He responded, "I don't know how to explain it. I just have this sense that God wants you to know you're going to see a miracle."

I smiled and tried to allow the excitement to replace my doubt. After all, we were gathered in the name of the Lord. We had only the desire to listen to him and do his holy will. With that I began to trust, not knowing where or when that miracle would happen, but I was excited nonetheless.

Seconds later, Jan stood up. Her face was visibly wet with tears, which were cascading down onto her already soaked blouse. They even fell onto the bible she clasped tightly in her hands. Her voice cracked through the emotion. "I want to give testimony to the presence of God here," she said with a trembling voice, "by telling you all what just happened to me."

"As I was sitting here, I was convinced that God was not part of any of this. As people were raising their hands, singing praise, speaking words from scripture, and sharing testimonies about what God had done for them, I really felt it was just a big put-on."

Jan's eyes, still filled with tears looked at us as she spoke, "My heart was very sad for all of you, and I just wanted to get out of here as fast as I could," she confessed. "I thought it was all fake, and just a lot of emotionalism."

"But then I looked down at my bible and opened it up to my favorite twenty-third psalm. As I read the words, 'The Lord is my shepherd; I shall not want,' I said to him, 'If you are really here Lord, then have someone say this,'" she said, showing the bible in her hand as proof. "When Charles said, 'I am your shepherd; you shall not want,' I knew the Lord was speaking directly to me," she concluded, glancing my way.

Suddenly, it all made sense! The Lord didn't need me to understand what he was doing. He only needed me to cooperate by saying the exact words he had given me to say. Those words were not, "The Lord is my shepherd; I shall not want," but rather, "I am your shepherd; you shall not want."

In that moment, those words were specifically meant for Jan, but they were also meant for all of us. Why? Because he loves us and wants us to know he is with us.

SEVEN

Reveal Yourself to Me

Two years after the birth of Micah, Mary again became pregnant with our second son, Joshua. Just as it had happened with Adam's pregnancy, Mary began to experience early contractions. We were on edge as they began, remembering the sadness of the son we lost. Like a bad recurring nightmare, Mary and I once again rushed to the hospital, seven months into her pregnancy.

Mary was quickly admitted as a patient and wheeled into the labor and delivery wing. They hooked her up to all sorts of machines, and I remember watching the line on the contraction monitor as it went up and down. I kept in constant contact with members of our prayer group throughout the ordeal, and it gave me great peace to know they were praying for us.

Joshua was born two months premature. Mary and I watched and prayed as his little body struggled for each breath in the NICU. After only four short days of improvements, however, we brought him home. Micah had a brother, and we were now a family of four!

I had two beautiful boys, my business finally was growing, and we were all healthy and happy. We felt truly blessed beyond measure as we continued growing in our faith.

I began diving heavily into scripture, and through scripture, God uncovered answers to questions that had become mountainous over the years. I had had so many unanswered questions throughout my years growing up Catholic, which had stacked up to an insurmountable height, initially causing me to question and doubt the faith.

As I continued to attend church with my family, I could see the goodness in it and the fruits it was producing in our lives. I found that the more time I spent with scripture, the more I was being drawn to the pew. Now that I was submissive to the Lord and surrounded by holy Catholic brothers and sisters, my faith at last began to take root and flourish.

Finally convicted that the Catholic Church held the fullness of truth, I wanted nothing but that truth. Moved to this conclusion, I knew what I needed to do. I needed to go to him, to *physically* face God in his *physical* church.

The next day, I parked in the empty lot at St. Margaret's Catholic Church and slipped through one of the heavy back doors. The church seemed large and solemn as I slid into one of the long wooden pews. After situating myself, I began to gaze upon the crucifix hanging above the altar.

As a bride lifts her veil to reveal her most beautiful face to her bridegroom, the Lord revealed himself to me there. In that moment, I realized that I was in absolute astonishment and awe of him. I was seized by him and overcome by a warmth and welcoming love that almost melted me.

In that moment, I was in the warm embrace of the Lord. Then I heard him speak softly to me, *"Welcome home."*

As I left the church and returned to my car, I was filled with the unquenchable love of Christ, certain of the truth of the Catholic Church. My soul had been strengthened by his word, and I could allow this faith to take root in my life and in our strong community of prayer and brotherhood.

Jesus was now incredibly real and personal to me. I talked to him and watched for him to act daily in my life. I found myself asking him to reveal his hand in all things to me, as his disciple. There were no more barriers or limitations on my faith. I was all in, ready for anything, and I longed to become a part of his mission!

As you can imagine, I was consumed with the zeal of St. Paul, as many converts have found themselves through the ages. I made it my greatest desire to see God, face to face. Yes, I was ready! I was hungry to set my eyes upon the God whom I saw so clearly in my spirit. It was time for a divine appointment, and I knew I had to prepare myself for this life-changing opportunity.

The question was not if, but when God would reveal himself to me. And so, I watched and waited, leaving the literal and figurative door open to him. Night after night, as I prayed in the silence of my bedroom, the door would remain open just a crack, allowing a single stream of light to shine in. I did this with the absolute expectancy that he would come through this light.

As I waited quietly, Mary usually was going about her business, cleaning up the dishes, and preparing the children for bed. She was happy to know that I was taking personal time in silent prayer. Had she known the true nature of my prayer, she surely would have thought I was nuts.

Then one night, as I knelt beside my bed in fervent prayer and expectation, I felt a serene stillness. I closed my eyes tightly, barely peeking through my eyelids. It suddenly occurred to me that I was apprehensive about what I might see.

But alas, this was it! The moment was here. A moving shadow cast its presence over me as it passed and came nearer. Suddenly, a dark mass rose and landed before me, only inches from my face.

My eyes shot open as I tried to control my racing heart. The dark mass, however, was not at all divine, but rather a furry and hissing cat. In my quiet meditation, he had stealthily entered the bedroom and jumped onto the bed, just inches from my face.

I cannot tell you the fear that pesky ball of fur inflicted on me that night. Shaking off the fright and embarrassment, I jumped up screaming, *"Why would you allow this to happen to me, Lord? You nearly scared me to death."*

As I stood there like a fool at the foot of the bed, with my eyes looking toward heaven, I heard the Lord say to me, *"If you really saw me in your present state, you would surely die of fright. You are not ready to experience that."*

Stunned and silent, I thought, "Wow! Could it be that the Creator of the universe used my cat, of all creatures, to convey this message to me?" In his magnanimous mercy (and his great sense of humor), he had spared me from a fear that would have killed me, and yet he answered me all the same. I believed and was thankful for his mercy. This would not stop me from pursuing him, however, as I was still endlessly curious and stubborn.

After this humbling lesson from the Lord, I knew I would not see him directly. But I also knew that I had heard him speak several times, and therefore I surely would encounter him again. I longed for this, and I began to pray often, asking for a concrete sign of his presence.

As I drove by myself from work to and from the weekly prayer meetings, I pleaded with the Lord to show himself to me in another form. "Lord," I asked, "could you not show yourself to me as a light, maybe on the side of the road or even at the top of a hill? I could handle that kind of a sign, and I would not be afraid."

Over the next few months, I drove back and forth on that same road, always searching for my burning bush. If nothing else,

I was confident he would reveal himself to me through some sort of light.

And then one night, I finally found him. It was not in the way I had expected or even anticipated on those many drives. Far off in the distance, I saw a red light on top of a hill. As I approached, it became bigger and bigger. Questioningly, I asked, "Lord, surely you wouldn't show yourself to me through a red light, would you?" It seemed strange, perhaps, because red reminded me of Satan, and I associated it with evil.

Yet, I listened for the Lord and kept driving toward the light. It was emanating from a house in the distance. As I got closer, I could see that the ruby glow was coming from a rooftop. One side of the roof to the other had been adorned in lights, forming huge red letters. To my surprise, the entire roof of the house was emblazoned with one word... JESUS!

I stopped my car immediately and got out. The same supernatural confirmation washed over me as I stood there next to my car. I was humbled in that moment, and I knew it was the Lord.

Once again he answered my call, even revealing himself on that road in the form of a light. The name "Jesus," in bright red lights across the roof of that house was unmistakable. "Thank you, Lord," I whispered. "The people who live in this house must love you, evident in their public witness. I'm sure they had no idea what putting your name on their roof would mean to a complete stranger when they did it, but you knew, Lord."

The family in that home was probably just getting an early start on Christmas decorating for the season, but I knew that God did this for me, to let me know how much he loves me, by answering my prayer.

> *"You will seek me and find me; when you seek me with all your heart, I will be found by you, says the Lord."*
> *(Jeremiah 29:13-14)*

I continued to pursue the Lord with all my heart. Eventually his hand in all things became as clear to me as those red lights. He continued to allow me to see his work and sometimes even participate in it.

EIGHT

Lord, Please Save My Father

It was early on a Sunday morning as I sat in the comfortable high-back sofa chair in our living room. Mary was upstairs getting the boys ready for church, and I decided to spend a couple minutes in prayer. As I sat there, the thought of my father crept into my mind.

My dad had passed away six years prior, and I deeply regretted not having the opportunity to share my experience of Christ with him before he died. He was the one man who always showed me love and compassion, but he certainly wasn't a follower of Jesus. He strayed from his Catholic faith and into bizarre Eastern religious practices that eventually led him into the occult.

He became a follower of Western esotericism, embracing spiritualism and the New Age movement. He spoke of everything from secret knowledge to UFOs. His extreme search for spiritual clarity and peace drew him deeply into the spiritual practices of yoga, and he eventually became a yogi. He started standing on his head and meditating, and he became a dedicated vegetarian; the traditional diet inextricably associated with enlightenment.

I would come home from work at night, and there he was, standing on his head in the corner of the living room. Apparently he was meditating on the inner eye, which somehow gave him a perception beyond natural sight. Somewhere along the line, Dad had gotten so misguided on his search for the divine, and that cursed path drew me in as well.

If only I could now share with him the truth in Christ and help release him from those many evil practices. But Dad had been spiritually lost long before he knew death in his physical body, and sadly I believed without a doubt that my father died in a state of mortal sin, which meant only one thing–hell.

As tears began to stream from my eyes at the thought of my dad's certain eternal fate, I remembered Luke 1:37, *"For with God nothing will be impossible."* I knew this was true, but what could it possibly mean for a man already dead? "Lord, can you save my father?" I asked.

And as I waited for his response, I heard him say, *"Don't hate your Uncle John."*

Shivers went up my spine at the mention of his name. Uncle John and Dad had been very close, but it was he who led my father into the occult in the first place. In fact, no one could get as close to my Uncle John as my father, and they would spend hours together dreaming of future endeavors.

My uncle had bought a small piece of land, and together he and my dad were going to grow and can foods. Uncle John planned to construct a fine home on the land according to the tenets of their shared beliefs, whatever that meant.

As the dangers of the occult became more evident to me, I became angry with Uncle John for leading Dad spiritually astray. Mary and I tried not to show our anger toward him whenever we encountered him at family gatherings, but it was certainly seething within. "Could God really be asking me to reach out to him now?" I wondered. I had to find out why God was asking me to lay down this anger.

I ran to the bottom of the stairs and called up to Mary, trying to sound as nonchalant as possible. "Hey, Honey, how would you like to go visit my Aunt Amelia and Uncle John after Mass?"

I was sure she would send daggers down the stairs with her eyes and refuse flatly, but to my surprise, she responded, "That's funny. I was just thinking about going to see your aunt and uncle." I looked up at her with a questioning glance, to which she casually added, "You know we've never even seen their new house."

"Okay, you have my attention, Lord," I thought as I walked back over to the chair and sat down again. At that moment, I knew something big was about to happen, and I could only follow where I was being led.

When we reached my uncle's house after Mass, I caught sight of him in the garage fixing his lawn tractor. Seeing Mary and me with the two boys, he began yelling for his wife at the top of his lungs, like a lunatic. My panicked aunt came running out of the house, expecting to find him trapped under the mower. Seeing the cause of the commotion, she chastised him and invited us in.

As we entered the house, we came face to face with a beautiful stained glass divider of Leonardo da Vinci's *The Last Supper*. Shocked to see anything religious in their home, I asked, "What's this?"

My uncle looked proudly upon the stained-glass faces of the disciples gathered around the table of Christ before responding, "Your father and I actually came up with this idea when we were planning the house I would build. We wanted this image to be the first thing anyone saw upon entering!" This seemed strange for the two of them, but I shrugged it off as a nod to a famous piece of artwork.

I walked into the kitchen where my aunt had begun cooking spaghetti. Oddly enough, from where I was standing, I also noticed a bible on a small table. At this second indication of Christ's presence within their household, my heart began to soften.

I had never known my aunt and uncle to be as kind and loving toward Mary and me as they were that day. As we gathered around the table to eat, my uncle blurted out, "You know, I really loved your father. Mike was the kindest man I ever knew." Uncle John started to get choked up as he laughed, "We would sit on the grass for hours, talking about how we would be independent of the world. We were going to grow our own crops, raise animals, and store the food for years to come!"

His laughter quickly faded into sadness, however, as he went on. "When Mike got stomach cancer, I tried everything I could think of to heal him. I called a Christian Science practitioner, we tried awakening his primal energy through Kundalini, unblocking his chakras, and even visiting Mount St. Mary's in Emmitsburg to drink the water from the spring."

"What did I just hear?" I thought to myself. In the midst of all that voodoo, did he really just say Mount St. Mary's?" My heart jumped inside of me at the mention of it. Suddenly, amidst all the entwined evil and darkness, there was a small glimmer of hope.

"Tell me more about that trip," I quickly pleaded.

Uncle John thought back fondly as he obliged. "There was a wonderful priest who said Mass, and afterwards he invited all lapsed Catholics in need of healing to come forward to the altar." Now I was truly on the edge of my seat, wondering how I had never heard of this trip.

"Your father slowly made his way up the aisle to the altar, and there the priest did something truly amazing. He asked all the men and women who had come forward if they would repent. Your father most humbly repented and upon doing this, the priest forgave his sins, administered the sacrament of Extreme Unction, and allowed him to receive Holy Communion!"

I felt both disbelief and euphoria as I heard these words drip like honey from my uncle's tongue. Baffled, I wondered how God answered a prayer like this, which I only had asked hours before. For six years, I had believed my father was lost. And then, once again, I remembered Luke 1:37, *"For with God nothing will be impossible."*

But there was more to come.

Many years later, Mary and I attended our first Catholic Charismatic Conference, which was held in Atlantic City, New Jersey. The place was packed beyond belief. Hotels were at maximum capacity, and every restaurant in town boasted lines that went on for blocks. Our small group happened upon a small Italian restaurant. The entire place only held about thirty people, and the old man in a tank top and apron who greeted us at the door seemed overwhelmed.

"What are all you people doing here?" he asked. "There is no way I can feed everyone," he added in an exasperated tone. Looking back into the kitchen area, I saw the restaurant staff–just two old men playing cards and drinking wine. It looked hopeless.

Quickly figuring out the situation, one lady in our group piped up, suggesting to the man, "Why don't you just sit down and relax? We can take care of this!"

I think he was just as surprised as I was by her boldness, as she shoved past him and made her way into the kitchen, followed by most of the women and several of the men in our group. The kitchen came alive with the banging of pots and pans as the women got to work cooking sauce, making meatballs, and boiling spaghetti. In the dining room, the men were cleaning tables, making drinks, and laying out silverware. A few of the men even began collecting money and putting it into the cash register.

When the first crowd of people eating at the restaurant left, another came right behind them, and then another, and still another. The whole time, our group worked the restaurant as if we'd worked there for years.

By the end of the night, the cash register was so packed with bills that it wouldn't close. Before we left, the women in our group made sure the restaurant owner and his two friends were well fed and the place was spotless. The old man dreamily stared out the door after us, calling, "Please come back again, and God bless you all!"

I think the charitable service that night spoke volumes to who we were–we were the hands and feet of Christ. The conference had been a true blessing, both in and out of the formal meetings. When at last we crossed the street to attend the final Saturday evening Mass, I was awed from my balcony seat by the sheer number of faithful participants filling the massive arena.

As the doors opened and the procession began, priests and deacons by the hundreds walked onto the stage toward the altar. I remember the music ministry playing "The King of Glory Comes," and as far as I was concerned, Jesus was processing in at the end of that line.

In reality, it was Bishop Nicholas D'Antonio closing the line. He would be saying the Mass and giving the homily. Bishop Nicholas was a Franciscan missionary priest who grew up in Baltimore, but found himself serving in the backcountry of Honduras, living among the peasants. Because of his push for just land reform, the Church and government remained at odds in his diocese.

His homily was captivating. We listened on the edge of our seats as he spoke of his 1975 trip to Rome, during a time when tensions were really growing in his diocese in Honduras. While he was away in Rome, several gunmen planning his death, instead killed two of his priests and twelve civilians, throwing their bodies into a well and blowing it up. This painful reality made him aware of what many Catholics face in other countries.

Due to the certain danger he would face upon returning to Honduras, his superiors transferred him to New Orleans. Although it was hard to leave Honduras, Bishop Nicholas found great joy working with Spanish-speaking Catholics in New Orleans. He encouraged us to have a heart for the poor and to work toward social justice for those who are oppressed and without a voice or moral conscience.

As he held up the host during the Consecration, he used his gift of tongues to praise God, who was now present in the Eucharist. From my balcony position, I could see waves of people with hands and faces raised toward the sacrifice of the altar. A scripture came to me in that moment from John 3:8, *"The wind blows where it wills, and you hear the sound of it, but you do not know whence it comes or whither it goes; so it is with everyone who is born of the Spirit."*

Suddenly the people below me appeared to form a field of grass, bending and swaying in unison with the wind of the Holy Spirit as they praised the Eucharist, yet unaware of this unison. It was a beautiful and heavenly sight to behold.

After the conference, Mary and I had a peaceful journey home, and I was excited to share our experiences with my mom. I knew I had to tread lightly, because Mom often felt I was overwhelming the family with miracles and came on too strong at times concerning the Catholic faith. But I felt this conference and the homily that inspired me was something Mom could both appreciate and understand.

"Mom, the Charismatic Conference was wonderful!" I began. "You should have seen the hundreds of priests, deacons, and nuns who attended as well. It was really awe-inspiring." Mom smiled politely as I went on, "And the Mass was so moving. Bishop Nicholas D'Antonio celebrated, and boy, did he have a story!"

Mom looked at me quizzically at the mention of the Bishop's name, hardly hearing another word I said. "Did they call him Bishop Nick?" she interjected, recalling a forgotten memory.

"What? Who? I'm not sure. Why?" I responded abruptly.

"Wait here," she instructed. "I have something to show you." With that, she scurried off down the hallway and into her bedroom. She returned a few minutes later, holding a small black binder as if it were sacred. She gently passed it to me.

I opened to a letter protected in a plastic sleeve. "Dear Josephine," it read. "I need you to know that I stopped at the hospital to see Mike before he died. We spoke together of many things, and I heard his confession. Please tell your sons for me that Mike is truly healed, and that he awaits us in heaven with Christ." The letter was from Bishop Nicholas D'Antonio.

As my mind once again flashed back to my prayer asking Jesus if he could save my father, I began to weep.

"Mom, why didn't you ever show this to me?" I demanded. "I didn't even know Dad knew Bishop Nick," I said, grasping at straws.

"Oh, your father and the Bishop were very close," she said plainly. "They were childhood pals. In fact, Bishop Nick was staying with mutual friends when your dad was in the hospital. When they told him, he rushed there straight away to give him his last rites."

My mind began racing a million miles a minute. "This couldn't be," I thought. I was there at my father's side when he died. I then recalled that my father, the dedicated vegetarian, had asked me if I thought it was okay for him to eat a hot dog. When I answered "Sure," to his strange request, he asked me to get him one from the hospital cafeteria. I obliged, but when I returned, he was unconscious and died about ten minutes later.

Then it hit me. It finally clicked! My father had repented at Emmitsburg and had come back into communion with the Church. His last act of repentance, in the presence of the son he drew into the occult, was in turning away from his vegetarianism. This was his public witness to me, in rejecting his New Age beliefs.

What I didn't know was that in the time I spent in the cafeteria, Bishop Nick had been with my father, giving him his last rites. God had sealed his promise upon my heart; my father was with him in heaven.

To this day, the revelation of my father's salvation is the greatest miracle of my life! In sharing it with others, it has given many people hope and courage, as they too have asked God's mercy upon loved ones who they fear have passed in a state of debilitating sin.

I have revisited this miracle many times in prayer, giving Jesus great thanks. God can do all things from the wellspring of his divine mercy, which is timeless, never-ending, and incomprehensible.

> *"Let him return to the Lord, that he may have mercy on him, and to our God, for he will abundantly pardon. For my thoughts are not your thoughts, neither are your ways my ways, says the Lord." (Isaiah 55:7-8)*

NINE

The Gift of Aaron

When Mary and I envisioned our future together, we always dreamed of having many children sitting around our table. We could just see our large family growing throughout the years, filling our home with laughter and joy.

Like clockwork, two years after we welcomed Joshua into the family, Mary again became pregnant. We were sure it was another boy. I should mention that Mary only wanted sons, and she prayed fervently for this intention.

You can imagine how excited Micah and Joshua were to have another brother on the way. And yet, just five months into the pregnancy, Mary experienced a placental abruption. This is a rare and serious condition in which the placenta detaches from the wall of the uterus. It was so severe in Mary's case that she nearly died from the massive loss of blood.

Once again, we lost our baby, and almost his mother as well. It was a frightening experience for me, especially with two young sons. I couldn't imagine our life without Mary.

After a few days, Mary regained stability. Her doctor came into the room gravely and explained to us that he had given Mary a medication to stop the bleeding, which also had destroyed her gall bladder. He then poignantly clarified the severity and risk of Mary's current condition, and turning to me he said, "If she were my wife, I would never let her get pregnant again. If she does, she most likely will die."

His words chilled me to my core. I felt panicked and in some way responsible for her near-death experience. I had to take matters into my own hands, making sure we never found ourselves in this situation again.

It's important to note that Mary and I were using artificial contraception to space our pregnancy, which is intrinsically at odds with Catholic Church teaching.

I still didn't have *"church"* in my heart at this point. I treated faith like a buffet, picking and choosing what practices I did and didn't want on my plate. I wasn't yet a man who stood firmly on *all* the teachings of the Church. So, in my fear and anxiety, I said to Mary, "I think we need to get your tubes tied as soon as possible. Or perhaps I need to get a vasectomy." I knew I needed to do something permanent to make sure we were incapable of conceiving new life.

Mary, however, was not fully convinced. Although we were using artificial contraception, she could not imagine fully removing God from the equation by eliminating the possibility of another pregnancy altogether. This stance was formed especially in light of the miracles we were experiencing through our prayer group.

Mary's sister Rose and her husband Bob were practicing Natural Family Planning, a method approved by the Church. She decided she needed to learn more about it from Rose before making any permanent and irreversible decisions. I, on the other hand, felt that a natural alternative was far too risky and irresponsible, principally considering the gravity of another pregnancy for us.

We were at an impasse, and so I turned to the Lord. I found a quiet spot where I could be alone with him, and there I bowed my head. As I sat in my helpless despair and desperation, the Lord spoke to me. *"Stop using the foam,"* he said. His answer was clear. And yet, as he continued, I could not have prepared myself for what he would say next. *"It is the poison that killed two of your sons."*

My knees weakened as the magnitude of his words sank in. I felt unable to catch my breath, as if I had just received a hard blow to the gut. "Could Mary and I really be culpable for the death of our two miscarried sons, through our own ignorance and disobedience?" I thought. And yet, I knew it was true. Despite our ignorance and clouded vision, the Lord's words were true.

Tears ran warmly down my cheeks as I felt the healing embrace of mercy surround me. I had been forgiven before even asking for forgiveness. Then the Lord said, *"Begin using a method approved by the Church."*

This was going to be a real challenge for us. At the very point when another pregnancy could put Mary's life in jeopardy, the Lord convicts me to stop using contraception? This seemed crazy. But again I had to surrender, and the truth is, in my heart of hearts, I knew it was right.

After all, wasn't it God who first gave life to Mary, to me, and to all of our children (living and in heaven)? Wasn't it God who loved us in all things, always wanting the best for us? Who were we, then, to put a permanent restriction on him in bringing forth new life? This was God! It's who he is and what he does. God brings forth life. Yet, I still had fear in my heart at the thought of surrendering Mary's life for his sake.

Mary was delighted when I came to her in great humility and surrender, telling her I was finally on board with beginning the Natural Family Planning method, rather than continuing artificial contraception. She met with Rose and began learning all the details of the practice, and for a short time things seemed to be going rather well.

And then one evening, Mary came to me with an earth-shattering announcement. "Honey," she said gently, "I'm pregnant." As she said the words out loud, a look of fear came over her face. I just stared at her, watching the storm cloud overshadow her, and I truly was devastated.

"This is my fault," I said with furrowed brow, trying not to cry. "I should have had a vasectomy," I added angrily. Then in a whirlpool of emotions, I said, "I can't lose you. My boys need their mother!" I was willing to do anything. I would have sold my soul to save her.

And so, I suggested she have an abortion. Mary looked at me with a saintly calm. The storm had passed in her, and she was somehow filled with peace and clarity now.

"No," she said firmly. "I will not abort my baby." Then she said softly, "I will gladly die so that he can live."

"How could she say that? How could she think that? What about me? What was I going to do?" I felt desperately alone in my agony and despair, which would quickly become worse when we returned to face Mary's doctor with this news.

I felt sick to my stomach as he shot me a look as if I had killed Mary in cold blood. His face became red with anger as he started to shout at us. Then, at the end of his rant, he paused for a few moments, considering the true gravity of the situation. His voice was no longer driven by anger, but rather it took on a similar despair to mine. He swallowed hard and then said to us, "I am Catholic and will never perform an abortion." I stood silently as Mary looked instantly in his eyes, firmly declaring, "I don't want one."

I reflected in that moment on how women are said to be selfish and cowardly in choosing to continue a pregnancy that could end their life, leaving their families without them. There was no greater falsehood. I was sure that Mary was the strongest and most valiant woman that had ever lived. Her courage shined brightly over both my own cowardice and the doctor's anger. He lowered his head for a moment and then said, "I will do everything I can to save you and this baby." Mary was at peace, but his words did nothing to comfort me.

The weeks dragged on agonizingly for me as I implored the Lord for an answer, hoping to hear his voice. Mary and I went to a prayer service with her parents at Most Precious Blood Church, and I was drawn to the young charismatic priest who led it. His faith and contagious joy were inspiring, and so I pulled him aside after the service to talk about what Mary and I should do.

Knowing the Church's teachings on contraception and abortion, I had a pretty good idea what he would say, but for some reason I needed to reconcile it with my conscience. I was desperately seeking the face of God's mercy.

Recounting Mary's history to him, I said, "I know it's not right to terminate the pregnancy, but another pregnancy could kill her, and I need an answer." Father thought for a moment and then looked up pensively at me before saying, "I can't give you an answer on this. This is your decision to make." That was it. I was left just as helplessly directionless as before I had come.

When we returned home from the prayer service that night, I went into our basement and got on my knees. I needed the darkness and the quiet stillness to be alone with the Lord. I cried out loud to him like David in the psalms. "Lord, I am terrified," I shouted. "You told us to stop using foam contraception, and now Mary is pregnant. Tell me what to do."

I would not be silent, and I would not stop crying out to him and seeking him until he gave me an answer. "Lord," I pleaded, "I need your peace, which passes all understanding." As I sat quietly and listened for the Lord, I could feel myself becoming more and more desperate.

Then, breaking through my anxiety was the now familiar voice of peace. The Lord said, *"I will tell you what to do from the altar on Sunday at Mass."*

Finally, an answer! I jumped up and ran all the way upstairs, shouting to Mary. "He spoke to me! He spoke to me!" I practically screamed. Mary laughed as she beheld me, running and shouting like an excited child.

"Calm down, and tell me," she said, trying not to let her amusement show.

"The Lord is going to reveal the answer to us on Sunday from the altar," I gasped, trying to catch my breath.

"Okay," she accepted with a thoughtful look.

My excitement was bubbling over as I went on to say, "We will sit in the very first row at church and listen attentively to everything that is said!"

On Sunday morning, I flew out of bed and anxiously rushed everyone into their clothes and out the door. I had never been so excited to go to Mass. We got there early, and I marched us directly up the center aisle and into the first pew. I sat there listening diligently, hanging on every single word that was uttered from the altar.

When the time came for the Old and New Testament readings, I turned excitedly to Mary. "Listen," I said, "this is it!" But as the lector concluded the first reading, I heard nothing directional regarding our particular situation. Turning to Mary once again, I reassuringly said, "It'll probably be the second reading, or the Gospel."

We listened to the New Testament reading, but again, nothing related to our issue. When the Gospel reading finally had been proclaimed and still nothing made sense to us, my head dropped, and I became truly embarrassed and devastated.

My heart sank further as the priest finished his homily, closed the bible, and walked back toward his seat. I couldn't take my eyes off him, hoping for something more. And then, in a moment of clarity and realization, he turned and walked back to the podium. He unfolded a piece of paper that had been placed inside the podium, and drew his lips once again to the microphone.

"Excuse me," he said, addressing the congregation. "I was supposed to read this statement from the Holy Father today." His eyes scanned the declaration as he read, "For no reason whatsoever should abortion be considered as an alternative." With that, he refolded the paper, returned it to its place in the podium, and then walked to his seat.

Looking over at my beautiful wife, filled with every confidence in God and his providence, I almost jumped up and shouted, "Amen!" Now I knew that he was in control. Not only in control of my life, but also of this very pregnancy and Mary's life as well. *Nothing* was going to happen without his divine hand directing and allowing it to be. Finally, I had found the same peace that Mary had discovered very early on.

As the months went by, Mary and I were filled with joy. Her pregnancy was seemingly perfect. Then came month seven, and we were again tested, as early contractions led to another emergency hospitalization. Our doctor was wonderful, and between his medical expertise and the prayers of the community, Mary's contractions subsided, and she was released.

Right at the nine-month mark, Mary's contractions started normally and on schedule. We excitedly rushed to the hospital, and as she was wheeled into the delivery room, I was escorted into the waiting room. Looking around at the large crowd of expectant fathers, I had the feeling it would only be minutes before my baby was born. A nurse soon confirmed this, coming into the waiting room to report, "Mr. Piccirilli, your wife is starting to dilate quickly, so it won't be long now."

I was permitted to go back and see Mary briefly before she began hard labor. "I better call Rose," I said to Mary. "She should know what's happening." Mary told Rose absolutely everything, but surprisingly she said, "No, let's wait until the baby is really ready to come." With that, I headed back to the waiting room.

This was 1976, and in those days, no one was allowed in the delivery room during labor until the baby was born, washed, and prepared. So, I paced back and forth in the waiting room, watching as one elated father after another was called from the room to go meet his new baby. Finally, I was the only one left.

At 6:30 a.m., more than thirteen hours after we'd arrived, I watched the door swing open once again, and I tried to read the expression on the nurse's face. She assured me that Mary was still dilating normally. At that point I thought, "The heck with this," and I ran to the phone to call Rose. Somehow I knew I needed her to be there.

Still to this day, I can't explain how Rose got to the hospital so quickly—at least not without a fleet of police cars chasing after her. She sat down next to me with an air of satisfaction, saying, "I'm so glad you called. I asked the Lord not to let this baby be born without me being here."

I stared at her with heavy bloodshot eyes. "What?" I said in exasperation. "If I had known that, I would have called you thirteen hours ago!" Just then we both heard the cry of a baby and strained to see down the hallway.

"Is that our baby?" Rose asked.

I looked around the empty waiting room before saying, "It has to be. No one else is here."

The nurse led us through the doors and down the hallway. Rose and I entered the room, and there was Mary cradling our beautiful new son, Aaron. He was perfect in every way, and so might I add was his mother. Mary shifted him into my arms, and as I held him next to me for the very first time, I felt united to my heavenly Father through an indescribable covenant. The child I now held in my arms and loved more than anything was almost never conceived, or given the chance to live, when I was in control. He was our miracle child, and I thank God for Mary's faithful obedience, God's word to me, and dare I say...the teachings of the Catholic Church!

One Sunday shortly after the birth of Aaron, Mary and I returned to that same front pew for Mass with our three boys, specifically thanking God for his love and grace upon us. As we sat there together, we heard someone shout out from the congregation, "See that baby? He's a miracle!" We swung our heads around to see where the voice was coming from.

Surprisingly, it was Mary's doctor–the same one who angrily feared we were making a grave mistake in our openness to another pregnancy. He had been attending our church and was just as moved by Aaron's miraculous birth as we were. When he saw us there with Aaron, he just had to shout out before the Lord in the witness of others that he had seen a miracle.

I went out and purchased a set of plaques to hang on the wall in our living room in celebration of our family. The main plaque was inscribed with our family name, Piccirilli, and the words from Joshua 24:15 under it: *"Choose this day whom you will serve, but as for me and my house, we will serve the Lord."* Under the main plaque, I hung three additional plaques with the names Micah, Joshua, and Aaron inscribed on them. As I hung the plaques, I felt overcome with pride in the Lord, and I felt truly blessed among men.

Yet, despite our overwhelming joy at the birth of our son Aaron, I still needed to revisit the Lord's devastating words to me about the loss of our other two sons and our willful disobedience to the teaching of the Church. This remained in the back of my mind for three years, when finally, it was brought to light.

I was sitting on our sofa in prayer, quietly listening to the Lord. He interrupted my current thoughts, speaking very clearly to me. He said, *"You are missing two plaques."* At first I was confused. After all it had been three years since I had hung the plaques on the wall, and I hadn't given much thought to them since.

"You have five sons," the Lord declared boldly to me. After a few moments of further confusion, I realized that the Lord was speaking of the two sons Mary and I had lost in miscarriage. I was flabbergasted; remembering once again the painful words the Lord had spoken to me three years earlier.

I asked Mary to sit down with me that night, mournfully asking her if she remembered the names we had intended to give our other two babies. Mary lowered her eyes and stared at the carpet at the mention of her sons, softly speaking the names she had not spoken in years. "Adam and Gabriel," she said solemnly.

Although we were never told the gender of our babies at the time, God said he gave us five sons. He had given Mary what she always wanted–all boys!

At last I understood and was compelled to respond to the Lord. I needed to make it known to him, and to my whole household for that matter, that I accepted the Lord's correction and was a repentant man. With that, I went out and purchased two more plaques.

Inscribed on the plaques were the names Adam and Gabriel. Returning home, I hung them on the wall directly above the main plaque, because our two sons were already with the Lord. From that point forward, I have acknowledged that I have five sons, two in heaven.

The Gospel of Luke 15:31-32 suddenly spoke to me very personally, regarding my own sons. It sounded like this: *"My three sons, you are always with me, and all that is mine is yours. It is fitting to make merry and be glad, for these your brothers were dead, and are alive; they were lost, and are found!"*

Mary and I had stopped acknowledging our two sons after losing them in miscarriage. But suddenly they were returned to us! We experienced the joyful realization that they would be with us again in heaven. They had not ceased to exist. Their souls were not reborn as other children. They were alive and well in heaven, with Jesus the King!

As soon as I hung the additional two plaques on the wall, Mary stepped back to look at them. Suddenly, she began to weep sorrowfully. I looked over at her tenderly, realizing she was finally allowing herself to mourn the loss of Adam and Gabriel.

PART TWO:

But
Now
I See

TEN

See God's Love in All Circumstances

One of the first things our prayer group did after deciding to become a covenanted community was to seek the Lord's direction for our vision and mission. We all had Christ in common, that much we knew. Catholics were Catholics, Lutherans were Lutherans, and non-denominational Christians were Christians just the same. We spoke of our differences, remaining true to the teachings of our own church. We all loved Jesus.

What God revealed to us was very simple and basic. Our vision was to see God's love in every circumstance, and our mission was to live that out, sharing it with others whenever we could. We were all in agreement on this, and so we adopted and tried to put it into practice.

You can imagine how incredibly challenging our lives became. Just picture someone saying, "I found out I have cancer. Praise God! Thank you for loving me through this cross, Lord." Or, "I lost my job and have no income at the age of fifty-eight, and with a family to support. Thank you, Jesus, because even in this circumstance, you are loving me!"

These responses certainly did not seem normal at first. And yet, we all believed in their truth. We knew definitively that God loved us, and therefore was somehow working for our good in every situation. For it is written, *"We know in everything God works for good with those who love him, who are called according to his purpose."* (Romans 8:28) And we knew we were being called according to his purpose.

Our community proceeded to cling to this scriptural promise even in the scary moments of life, encouraging each other to genuinely follow with the question, "Why are you allowing this happen to me, Lord?" This was not an angry demand of self-pity, but rather the humble question of a curious apprentice. In Matthew 26:40, Jesus asks Peter and the disciples, *"Could you not watch with me one hour?"* That's what we wanted; to remember that and learn from it.

Patiently, we watched for his answer in every moment, knowing that he loved us. Once intrinsically adopted, this new perspective began transforming us radically. Our anger, fear, anxiety, frustration, and doubt became unimportant. All that mattered was watching for God's answer.

This was, of course, in drastic contrast to the "I want it, and I want it now" mentality I was escaping. Suddenly in discipleship to the Lord, a deep humility replaced my former selfishness, for then I knew the Holy Spirit had been sent to comfort and guide us always to the truth. And so he did, answering us over and over again.

The first time I truly put this new way of thinking into practice was a memorable one. On a bright sunny morning as I made my way into work through the heavy traffic of Baltimore's St. Paul Street, I navigated the lanes of "breathing down your neck" traffic. The last thing I needed that hectic morning was the loud BANG that came from the engine of my car.

The car stopped dead, right there in the middle of traffic. Smoke was coming from under the hood, and my steering wheel was impossible to turn. As horns began blasting and drivers hollered expletives amidst nasty hand gestures, I felt smoke coming out of my ears as well.

One of my first thoughts was simply disbelief. "My new Ford's motor just blew up!" Then my frustration and anger began to build and increased by the moment. The smoking engine became like an active volcano, and I was stuck there in rush-hour traffic, surrounded by inconsiderate drivers who were about to experience my wrath.

But then, something just popped into my mind. "See God's love in all circumstances." Although this particular situation seemed to be getting worse by the minute, instead of shouting what I originally might have been inclined to shout, I started praying out loud, "Thank you Jesus, thank you! I praise your name for allowing this to happen to me." I'm sure if anyone had heard me, they would have thought I was mad, or at least incredibly sarcastic.

Sucking up my pride, I slipped out of the car and lifted the hood. As I surveyed the engine, I was surprised to see that my motor appeared to be fine. That's when I noticed a broken fan belt. Trying to figure out my next move, I saw that the belt to the left of the alternator was the same size as the broken one to the right of the power steering. So, I pried the left belt off with my tire iron and slipped it onto the right side. It fit like a glove!

Jumping back into my car, I started it right up and drove to the gas station to get a new belt. On the way, I really began thanking God and praising him for blessing me with an easily fixed car.

But I had the feeling that wasn't everything the Lord wanted to show me through the incident on St. Paul Street that day. So I continued "watching" throughout the day, asking the Lord why he allowed that to happen to me. I watched and waited for an answer all day, like a hungry bulldog waiting on a bone.

That evening Mary and I had an appointment with my brother Bud, who was a realtor, was supposed to be picking Mary and me up in his new camper. We were going to look at new homes. He was picking us up in his new camper van to look at new homes in Bel Air, Maryland, near our *New Life* community.

As we sat waiting on the front steps, we saw him walking up the road. "Bud," I shouted, "where's your van?"

Bud's face was caught somewhere between anger and despair. He frantically called back, "My new van's motor just blew up!" I knew that look on his face, I knew that panic in his voice, and I even knew that same car situation. In that instant, I also knew God's answer to my "why."

Walking up to my brother and putting my hand on his shoulder, I said with laughter in my voice, "Bud, God loves you very much!" Now, you can imagine his initial reaction, but I continued, "You see, your van's motor didn't blow up. It was just a fan belt that broke." I then confidently instructed, "I'm going to follow you back and get your tire iron, so I can switch it with a belt on the other side of your motor. Then, we can get you to a gas station and get a new belt."

Bud looked at me like I was an absolute lunatic. "Are you crazy, Charles?" he said. "I just told you my motor blew up. I can't drive the van. I drifted the thing to the side of the road, where it is sitting right now. I won't be taking anyone anywhere."

The gift of faith had soared into my heart at that moment. "Bud, take me to the van," I commanded. And yet, as we walked to the van, his doubt began to affect me. For a moment, I considered the fact that my Ford and Bud's van were completely different vehicles. I began to wonder if the problem truly was the same. I would look like a fool if this turned out not to be the case. In my heart, I whispered a prayer, saying, "Get behind me, Satan. This is God's work."

As Bud raised the small hood of the van, I had the reassuring confirmation that the motor was in excellent condition. And there, sure enough, was the broken fan belt! I asked Bud for his tire iron and repeated the same procedure I had performed earlier on my own car. As Bud turned the key in the ignition and the motor started, I felt the rush that comes only from the Lord.

"Wow, God," I thought. "You showed me why you let my car break down in the middle of St. Paul Street after all."

In fact, God had allowed Bud, Mary, and me to see his hand at work. He rewarded me for my trust in him and for my desire to see him move, even in the little things in my life. This was also a great confirmation for me of the philosophy the community had adopted. And of course, the Lord wanted my brother to know how much he loved him as well. What a wonderful gift that he let me deliver!

The lesson of Romans 8:28 again was proven to be true. The Holy Spirit was always reminding me of this, that all who are being called according to his purpose must watch for his love in every circumstance, even busted fan belts.

ELEVEN

Miracle Acres

As Mary and I continued to look for homes, believing that God wanted us to move closer to our *New Life* community, we began to pray together that the Holy Spirit would guide us and lead us to the right home.

I remember the many long afternoons spent in the car, driving around looking at properties, searching for just the right place. All the while, we were asking the Lord to confirm his will to us. Bud continued helping us with our search, but nothing he found ever panned out.

Finally, one of the houses we found was perfect! Mary and I were equally excited about it, and so we joined together in prayer, asking the Lord if this was "it."

We had budgeted and calculated, determining that the most we could spend was $60,000. I knew it was a low offer for the house we both loved, but I made an appointment with the owner anyway. After speaking with him briefly about the property, I gave him our max offer of $60,000. He laughed amusedly, before flatly responding, "no."

When I returned home and told Mary about his response, she understood and felt confident to move on. I, on the other hand, felt a bit dejected.

Oddly enough, the very next evening, there was a storm in which that house was struck by lightning. It set the whole roof ablaze. Mary and I were shocked by the news, remarking on the clarity of the "no" from the Lord, as well as from the owner.

The next day, Bud called to tell me about another amazing property he had found. "There is a farm in Bel Air," he said excitedly. "It's thirty-nine acres, has an Olympic-sized pool, three houses, twelve cabins, a lake, a vineyard, and a theater with a stage. It also has a huge two-story building with a community kitchen and a seating area for about forty people, not to mention an exposed fireplace!" he concluded, almost out of breath.

"You and Mary have to at least check this place out, even if you don't have the money to buy it," he insisted. I agreed, very interested in seeing a place like that and wondering how much it would go for.

I couldn't help but think how nice it would be to have something like that for our growing community. Realistically, though, the community was still small and didn't need all the amenities it offered. All Mary and I needed was a single-family home.

At the time, I had a mentor in our community who walked beside me on my spiritual journey. Charlie and I got along very well. When he inquired into our house search, I told him about the property Bud had found. He agreed that something like that sounded amazing for our community, but was probably way out of our price range. Still, the location wasn't far away, and he agreed to join me in checking it out.

As Mary and I followed the directions to the sale property, I paused for a moment and lifted my voice to the Lord. "Please Lord," I prayed, "give us a sign if we are meant to have this property for ourselves and our community." Even though it was beyond our financial reach, I couldn't help imagining how wonderful it would be, and perhaps even possible, if Charlie and I both chipped in.

As we finally turned the bend to enter the property, I saw a sign that said "Miracle Acres." I smiled from ear to ear, considering the irony of the "sign" the Lord had given us. "Look," I said to

Mary, "it's a 'sign' sign." Mary giggled her silly giggle, also excited when she read it.

"Oh, honey, I just know God is doing something," she whispered as she squeezed my arm.

We began walking around the extensive property of well-manicured grass, unable to believe how beautiful and well maintained it was. As we continued weaving in and out of the houses on the property, everything seemed oddly familiar to me, as if I had been there before.

Unable to shake the nostalgic feeling, I approached the auctioneer and asked him about the history of the place. He very excitedly recounted the property's past, telling me that it used to be a camp for city kids called the "Fresh Air Farm." I couldn't believe my ears. "The Fresh Air Farm?" I asked. "I came to The Fresh Air Farm with my brother when I was a boy!"

Driving home with Mary that day, I talked a mile a minute about how perfect Miracle Acres was. I knew my boyhood experience at the Fresh Air Farm was not being recalled in my adulthood as mere coincidence.

"Something is happening," I said to Mary enthusiastically. "We need to pray really hard and seek the Lord's face on this one, so he can tell us exactly what he wants us to do here." So, I prayed and prayed, knowing that in just two short weeks the property would be auctioned off!

And then, God answered my prayer. He opened my mind specifically to the story of Elisha in 2 Kings 6:15-19. The Aramean army was sent to capture Elisha, surrounding his camp with horses and chariots. When Elisha's servant asks, *"What shall we do?"* Elisha prays that God may open his servant's eyes to see the many horses and chariots of fire around Elisha.

When the Aramean army, at last, does come down the mountain
to seize Elisha, he prays for God to strike them with blindness.
Elisha says to them, *"This is not the way, and this is not the city;
follow me, and I will bring you to the man whom you seek."*
With that, the Arameans are led into captivity in Samaria,
where their eyes are once again opened.

After revealing this scripture to me, God said, *"I am going to
strike the buyers blind to the value of this property. I want you to
go and say, '$90,000 in Jesus' name.' With that, it will be yours."*

I couldn't believe it! Unable to shake my giddiness about the
property, I called Charlie to tell him what God had just said.
He was just as excited as I was. Having also visited and fallen
in love with the property, he assured me, "I will be right there
with you on auction day, and we can split the cost!"

I knew that Mary and I didn't have $90,000, but if Charlie and
I each put in $45,000, we could buy the property together, and our
families could live in two of the three homes on the property's
spacious campus.

When I told my sons that, "Daddy is going to say, '$90,000 in
Jesus' name,' they enthusiastically responded and wanted to come
along. I was happy to share this opportunity with them because
I wanted them to see the Lord's work in action.

That Saturday morning the boys and I went to the auction.
Our excitement mounted as I showed them around the beautiful
property, and once again felt overwhelmed at the thought of
this place becoming our new home. All the while I kept a close
lookout for Charlie, who assured me he would be there.

But as the minutes passed and it got closer to auction time,
I became increasingly nervous. Charlie still hadn't shown,
and I knew I needed both his support and the assurance of his
half of the money to make this thing happen.

The boys and I made our way over to the auction area, and I slumped down stiffly on the ground next to them, staring at the check in my hand, already written out for $90,000.

As the auctioneer walked to the front of the crowd to open the bidding, I could feel the drops of sweat creeping down the sides of my face. The auctioneer greeted the anxious bidders as I once again scanned the parking lot. "Okay," he said, "let's open the bidding at $300,000."

"$300,000!" I thought in panic. But then the words of the Lord returned to me, reminding me that he would strike the crowd with blindness. We all waited, listening to the silence. Not one person bid on the property.

The auctioneer looked a bit surprised that he would have to drop the bidding lower than the starting price. "$250,000," he proclaimed boldly, waiting to drop the gavel. But again, no one bid. "$200,000?" he said questioningly. Still no one bid.

I looked around the crowd anxiously. There was a realtor and about forty other people. Surely they knew how much this property was worth and what a magnificent deal they could get on it. I looked from the fast-talking auctioneer to the hungry crowd of property sharks, and finally to the faces of my young boys. They were staring at me eagerly, confidently waiting in anticipation for me to move. "Say it, Dad, say it!" they prodded.

But I allowed the voice of doubt to creep in and take over in that moment, and it became deafeningly overwhelming. "Where is Charlie?" I screamed inside my own head. "He's not coming, is he?" Drops of sweat continued to fall, and I was paralyzed.

And just like that, I was distracted from the promise of the Lord. I began to listen to the whispers in my ear masquerading as logical reason. "Can we really manage a property of this size anyway? After all, who's going to cut all this grass?" I thought.

Sinking in my seat, I frantically scanned the parking area one last time, hoping to catch sight of my friend. But with no sign of him and hope dwindling, I bowed my head in a prayer of sadness.

"Lord, I can't do it," I conceded. "I am terrified." Looking out of the corner of my eye at the check in my hand, it was eclipsed by the faces of my sons. I said, "Please let someone bid over $90,000."

After surrendering in fear before the Lord, I sat frozen for a moment or two as the auctioneer came all the way down to $110,000. Finally, a voice in the crowd called out, "$150,000!" The auctioneer looked at him in relief before dropping his gavel and shouting, "Sold!"

I sat deflated in my spot on the ground, wondering how I would explain to my sons that their dad had simply chickened out. Seeing the two men who owned the property, I couldn't help but approach them after the auction ended. When I asked them how they felt about the property selling so low, their answer shocked me. One of them graciously said, "We asked the Lord what we should accept for this property, and he gave us a bottom figure of $90,000."

It turns out that one of the men was a pastor and the other was a deacon at a local church. I was happy that the Lord had blessed them with an extra $60,000, despite my weakness. Yet, I knew the Lord had given this property into my hands. The response of the owners was only further confirmation.

I went home and begged God to forgive me. This time I was begging forgiveness for what I had not done. God in his tenderness and mercy did forgive me. The lesson he revealed was in his great ability to do anything, even bring blindness to a crowd fighting over a treasure.

I also learned an important lesson about how evil can consume our hope by whispering words of doubt to us. And yet, despite my weakness, God did not forget my repentance, and in his merciful generosity, he gave me a future blessing of the same $90,000.

When my three boys were growing into young men, Micah was beginning his search for a college. At this point, I was reminded of a pivotal moment during the Catholic conference Mary and I attended in Atlantic City, New Jersey.

At one point during the conference, a dynamic Franciscan priest had taken the stage. He spoke with a strong love and delivered such words of wisdom and teaching that I knew he was deeply touched by God. I remember him shaking and holding onto the podium as he said, "The Lord speaks; who will not listen?" His name was Father Michael Scanlan, and he was the new president of the Franciscan University of Steubenville in Ohio.

As Father Michael spoke, the Lord also spoke to me, saying, *"That is where I want you to send your sons."* He clearly revealed these words to me about the University, and I knew that someday my sons would go there. Because of this conviction, for many years thereafter, I told my sons that I would only pay their tuition for one college–Franciscan University of Steubenville.

Yet, as time and circumstances pass, so can the strength of our conviction, even when it's rooted in Christ. My conviction was put to the ultimate test when Micah finished high school and was offered a full-ride art scholarship to Towson University in Maryland.

I thought about what the Lord had said to me, and considered the fact that Franciscan University had no art program. There was also the daunting fact that we didn't have the money to send him to Steubenville. I finally decided we should take advantage of this gift of a full scholarship and let Micah go to Towson.

I can still hear the desperation in his voice, when six months later he called me at work from his dorm phone. "Dad, I'm not going to make it here," he stated clearly. "There is too much temptation.

I'm drinking, shooting pool all the time, and cleaning up my roommate's vomit."

I couldn't believe my ears. Micah's words shook me in the same way the Holy Spirit must have shaken Father Michael Scanlan to speak in Atlantic City, New Jersey. Which was the same day the Lord asked me to send my son to his college in Ohio. Before my son could say another word, I interrupted him, "Do you want to go to Franciscan University?"

Without hesitation, he answered, "Yes dad, please!"

Relief washed over both of us as I said, "Then pack your bags. It's done."

I hung up the phone and immediately called Mary. I instructed her, "Mary, call Franciscan University and make arrangements for Micah to attend the upcoming semester. We are sending him there, no matter what the cost." This time, I was not going to put the Lord's kindness to the test, especially not when it came to my son.

Mary responded with a frantic, "What?" She knew as well as I did that we didn't have the money.

"God told me to send my sons there, and we will have to trust him to show me where to get the money. Even if we have to sell the house and live in a trailer, Micah is going!"

So, Mary called the University, and despite it being mid-year, somehow everything worked out with the admission process. About a month later, we found ourselves driving our oldest child to Father Michael's little college nestled on an Ohio hill.

The University was close to Pittsburgh, and there was nothing around but steel mills, a very old motel, and a few stores. Driving up the long winding road to the top of the hill on which the campus rested, I felt as if we were driving on holy ground.

We arrived a day early, and the campus was dark and peaceful, covered in a thick blanket of snow.

When we knocked on a door below one of the dorms, a Franciscan friar in a long black habit greeted us. Inside the room, the friar instructed several young men to help unload Micah's things from the car. The guys hopped up right away and helped joyfully.

When the car was empty and Micah was settled into his room, the friar said to us warmly, "Don't worry, we'll take great care of him. In fact, we're just making some pies, if he wants to join us."

Micah couldn't say no to that! He turned to us, full of gratitude, and said genuinely, "Go home, I'll be just fine here." We saw how warm and welcoming it was, and we knew Micah would thrive there. Still, it was hard for us to leave.

During our six-hour drive back to Maryland, Mary and I did not speak one single word. I felt like my heart was being ripped from my body, and I could tell that Mary was crying into her handkerchief. It was heartbreaking to be so far from our boy, but we knew it was best for him. I fumbled with the radio until I found a Christian station, and we listened as the consoling words filled our car.

When we arrived home, a welcomed peace came over both of us. We knew Micah was in the palm of the Lord's hand, right where he was meant to be.

It wasn't until the next day at work that I seriously started thinking about finances and about how the Lord would help us pay for our children's education. I began praying intensely for this intention for the next several weeks. That's when I got an unexpected call from Greg, who was one of our customers. Greg had not been spiritually in a good place when we first met, but had a rather moving experience through our encounter, and he has treasured it ever since.

Years before, Greg had come into my office with a head full of
ideas for his company. He was explaining them all to me when he
abruptly was stopped dead in his tracks by a sign that hung above
my desk. It read, "Let Go, and Let God." For whatever reason,
this phrase struck him to his core and was exactly what he needed
to hear at the time. The Holy Spirit moved in him as he read those
words, and Greg had an internal transformation in that moment
that returned him to his faith and a life of virtue.

Now, as I greeted him on the other end of the line, he asked rather
spontaneously, "How much would you charge us to retain you for
doing all the work for our company next year?"

Perplexed, I asked, "What work?"

He started rattling off various printing jobs, slide shows, graphics,
and displays. I could hardly keep up with him. I began pricing
his company's current costs on top of the additional work he
wanted us to do. "I don't know if this is correct," I said finally.
"The figure I have right now is just an estimate." This was
not much of a concern to him. "Right now, it looks like about
$90,000," I said.

Immediately, he responded, "Send me a bill!"

So, I sent off the bill, and a few days later, I received a check
for $90,000. I called to ask Greg why he was doing something
like this–sending me a full payment for estimated work to be
completed in the following year. This was certainly not the norm,
and in fact, I had never had this happen before. He simply replied,
"I wouldn't do this for anyone else but you. God bless you,
Charles. Put it in the bank."

At the time, I didn't put two and two together about the
significance of the $90,000, the exact amount the Lord had
asked me to offer for the Miracle Acres property. It already had
been years since that day, and it wasn't until years later that I
finally made that connection. Rather subtly, the Lord revealed to

me how he had brought the $90,000 full circle, and I was blown away.

He blessed all of my children and me with that money. But, this time I was obedient to him. I was able to send all three of my sons to Franciscan University with the tuition money God supplied. There, the faith of my sons blossomed and thrived. Many lifelong friendships were formed, two of them met their wives there, and the extended blessings have been too numerous to count.

John 14:12-14 states, *"Truly, truly, I say to you, he who believes in me will also do the works that I do; and greater works than these will he do, because I go to the Father. Whatever you ask in my name, I will do it, that the Father may be glorified in the Son; if you ask anything in my name, I will do it."*

When the Lord tells us, *"Ask in my name,"* we must ask him what it is that he intends to do. Often he has already revealed what he will do, and then he slowly unfolds how he will accomplish it.

As you can see from this story, the Lord revealed his answers and even gave me clear directions, yet I was weak in carrying them out. Our conversation with him must be unending, and our eyes must be forever open to his work. Time and again he will show us how the tapestries of our lives are connected through his will.

TWELVE

At the Foot
of the Cross

One of the most profound and powerful experiences I've ever had was at the foot of the cross. But how could I, Charles Piccirilli, have been at Calvary two thousand years ago, at the foot of the cross of our crucified Lord? Allow me to tell you.

Father Donald Rinfret, S.J., was director of the Jesuit Seminary and Mission Bureau in Baltimore, and he was the spiritual director to a woman named Mary Ellen Lucas. It became known to our community, as well as to thousands upon thousands of others, that she bore the stigmata, the visible wounds of Christ.

The Vatican had appointed a priest to investigate Mary Ellen's case, and in the meantime, had given her permission to pray for others and speak at various parishes. She captivated audiences, holding healing services from Ireland to the Philippines. She spoke about Christ, the Eucharist, respect for the clergy, rejecting the ways of the world, and sharing a love of the sacraments. All the while, drops of blood would begin to bead up and trickle down her forehead.

Aside from this unexplainable phenomenon, Mary Ellen was said to emanate an overwhelming scent of roses. This odour of sanctity often is associated with the saints and the wounds of stigmata.

When I learned that Mary Ellen was to speak at our parish in Bel Air, I was more than curious to see her and hear what she had to say. Along with three friends, I found myself crowded among the doors at the back of the packed church. We stood stiffly against the wall and watched as she entered the door beside us, not but five feet away, to see if we could smell roses as she continued walking to the front of the church.

It wasn't until later when she began to speak, however, that I was overcome by the most powerful fragrance of roses. The fresh sweet smell seemed to engulf the three of us in the back of the church, and we looked at each other in utter amazement.

Not long after this powerful experience, I learned that Mary Ellen would be speaking again at Mount St. Mary's in Emmetsburg, MD. Those attending would be given the opportunity to have Mary Ellen pray for them as they came forward.

A husband and wife who attended our parish decided to drive out for that special prayer service. They moved forward to the front of the church like the parting of the Red Sea as the crowd separated. Mary Ellen had her hands outstretched to the woman and as she got closer, she saw blood on Mary Ellen's face and was overcome with the motherly instinct to hug her.

As they hugged, she patted Mary Ellen's back and then felt herself slowly begin to fall. She was instantly taken to the crucifixion, hearing the voice of Jesus say, "Don't leave me! I love you!" As the woman's husband and children watched, they tried to understand what God was doing.

After that event, the couple began coming to our community prayer meetings where the wife would often experience the same physical and emotional pain of the crucified Christ in front of us all. I was never quite sure what to make of it. On one such occasion however, we slowly gathered around her, making it a priority to continue directing our focus on the Lord, but also supporting her in prayer.

Suddenly the woman stopped crying and looked directly at me. "Everybody stop," she cried out, "Stop and pray for Charles." I looked around at the inquiring faces, and replied assuredly, "I'm okay." This time she shouted louder, "Pray for Charles now. Pray for Charles!" With that, the circle shifted toward me and all began to pray as the woman held my hand.

Looking around the circle of friends in dismay, what happened next is not short of supernatural. Suddenly, I was falling backwards as if in slow motion. Further and further I fell, until finally I landed on my back in wet sticky mud. I felt it pool around my arms and the sides of my body as I lay there, struggling to raise myself to a kneeling position. As I rose, I caught sight of the sky, which hung over me, dark and foreboding.

Shivers went up my spine, because I recalled seeing that same dark sky once before. The date was March 7, 1970, and I was on a fishing trip with my brother and cousins. We were in two small boats on the Susquehanna River, filled with the excitement of the day. To our shock and horror, the beautiful sky filled with darkness in an instant, and we clung to the sides of the boats as the winds grew and the water became very choppy. That was the day of a total solar eclipse, a day that was imprinted on my mind.

But now, as I knelt in the mud, my eyes traveled across the grim sky and finally rested on a tall wooden cross that stood next to me. There hung a man on the cross, and I knew it was Jesus. Kneeling there under his left side, I couldn't see his face, but still I knew it was he. As I took in the sight of his body hanging there, white, tortured, and void of blood, I could only recall a scene from the movie E.T., in which the extraterrestrial creature lay dying in a stream. This is how the skin of Jesus looked to me.

I stared up at his lifeless body, which hung painfully above me. I wanted to look away, but my eyes were transfixed. As I continued gazing at his limp head and neck, an overwhelming pain consumed my heart. As the pain took hold of me I began to cry and scream as loud as I could. I screamed to the heavens and demanded that the Father hear me.

"Please, God, stop! He has done nothing wrong," my voice rang out into the hollow sky. "I am the one who is guilty!" I confessed aloud. Then between sobs, I begged, "Please stop them from hurting him."

At that moment, I felt the soft touch of an arm wrapping around my shoulder in a gentle embrace. "It's okay, he loves you," the soft motherly voice whispered. My tears continued falling as the darkness and mud faded away.

Slowly opening my eyes, I realized that I was back at the prayer meeting. I was lying on my back on the carpeted floor, which only moments before had felt thick with mud. Looking up with hesitation, I saw only a ceiling and a room filled with light. I felt the warm tears stream down the sides of my face as two of the men lifted me up from the ground and walked me into another room. As the profound vision passed, and I began to reacquaint myself with my familiar surroundings, I could not control my pain and crying.

When I was safely in the privacy of a separate room, Ken, one of the prayer group leaders, asked me what had happened to me. As I tried to find the words to explain this incredible experience, I found it agonizing to recall. Through tears, I gravely described to Ken the lifeless body of Christ hanging on the cross before me. "It was like seeing my young, innocent son on that cross," I explained. "If my own son had been up there dying for me, I would have felt the same. And yet, it was more than that. It was as if my son was not only dying for me, but that he was reassuring me all the while, 'It's okay, Dad, it's okay. I love you.'" That was the level of pain to which I could most accurately compare it, to that of my innocent little boy paying for my sins.

Then, realizing how much time this incident must have taken away from the prayer meeting, I humbly apologized. It seemed as if I had been at the foot of the cross for hours, slowly taking in every sensation—the thick mud, dark sky, and rugged cross with the bloodless body of my Lord upon it.

Ken looked confused at my apology, saying, "But Charles, you fell down and we immediately picked you up. That was it. The whole thing only took a minute."

I stared blankly at him, trying to reconcile his words with my experience. "How could that be?" I thought, being truly dumbfounded.

And then I realized that in God there is no time, for God works outside of time. It's not outside of his power to work within our natural limits, allowing us to experience the supernatural. Although the whole event lasted only as long as it took for my body to fall to the ground, I had a long and conscious experience. This opened my eyes to the mercy that God is able to give at the moment of our own death, and the opportunity to experience a lifetime of love as we cry out for his mercy in mere moments.

The following month, I shared the whole powerful story with the prayer group. For nearly a year after my experience of being at the foot of the cross, I could not look upon the crucifix without crying uncontrollably. In those moments, which seemed like hours, I had been brought into the Passion. I was given the gift of sharing in Christ's sacrificial love, with all of its pain and suffering.

Yet, in the midst of the devastation, there was also a serene gentleness. Looking upon the crucified body of Christ and beholding his innocence, knowing that he willingly laid down his life for me, I saw his love—and in that truest of loves, I loved him more than I thought possible.

THIRTEEN

Just Show Up

My brief experience with Jesus on the cross had left an imprint upon my very soul, which changed the way I encountered others in the faith. I was able to allow gentleness and compassion to rule, where previously judgment had resided. The Lord gave me once again an understanding of the scripture verse of John 3:8, which I began to love exceedingly.

"The wind blows where it wills, and you hear the sound of it, but you do not know whence it comes or whither it goes; so it is with everyone who is born of the Spirit."

I stopped trying to understand and explain everything God was asking me to do, instead, I gladly followed with excitement, watching for the next miracle.

That's one thing he showed me in abundance—he is certainly not short on miracles. I find myself often standing in awe of the mystery of him, not knowing what to expect, and at the same time always expecting that it will be good. So it was when I was asked to pray with a young man, who had just been released from prison.

Mary's Uncle Joe and his wife had started coming to our prayer meetings. I liked Uncle Joe a lot. He was an older gentleman, full of fire and love. Uncle Joe had witnessed a few of the miracles that God had performed through me. He believed in the special gift God had given to me, so I became his "go-to guy" on many matters of faith.

One night, Uncle Joe asked if I would go with him to his friend's house in the city. The man's son had just been released from prison, and he wanted me to pray with the young man, hoping he might accept Christ.

I was surprised by the invitation. "Me, Uncle Joe?" I asked. "But I've never done anything like this before," I protested. I knew that I still didn't understand the bible all that well, and I wondered what I would say to a man just out of prison.

Uncle Joe shook his head and looked me sternly in the eyes. "I don't care," he said. "Just come with me. You're young, and so is he. Just tell him he needs Jesus!"

Early the next Saturday morning, I hopped into the passenger side of Uncle Joe's car and drove with him into Baltimore City. We caught the sunrise just as we pulled up in front of a small row house. I became increasingly nervous and apprehensive as we climbed the steps, and Uncle Joe knocked on the door.

A kind, elderly man greeted us, and as we entered his home, we noticed a woman who sat knitting in a rocking chair across the room. Using sign language, he spoke to her, and she responded in like manner. I assumed she was his wife until the man turned back to us and said, "Follow me. My wife is downstairs with my son."

My bible was under my arm, frozen to my side, as I followed Uncle Joe down the steps and into the basement. As we entered the basement we were brought before a woman lying on a couch, covered from foot to neck in blankets. The elderly man approached her carefully and then introduced her to us as his wife, sister of the lady in the rocking chair upstairs.

"My wife is very ill, you see," he said sadly. "She has not been able to move from this couch for over a month now." Uncle Joe and I exchanged a glance and then looked back at the man as he explained that his wife, also deaf and mute, has been in too much pain even to be touched. "She just remains here now, covered in blankets," he said.

I assumed she might be suffering from some form of shingles, and the woman's condition certainly seemed to complicate the couple's troubles. Yet, it was their son we had come to see. The man told us that his son was hiding in the basement kitchen where we couldn't directly see him.

All I could think was, "What am I supposed to do now, Lord?" This was certainly turning out to be an awkward situation, and I had no idea what Uncle Joe, or the Lord for that matter, had in mind. And yet, by now I had learned to follow the lead of the Holy Spirit, and this included walking into some very unusual situations.

Taking a moment, I decided to do what I always do when I'm not sure what the Lord is asking next. I knelt down in front of the woman, and bowing my head in prayer, I waited. In those moments, I listened intently for the words the Lord would give me to speak.

After a minute or two, I noticed that the woman was staring attentively at my face, trying to find the answer in my eyes. Watching my lips, I could tell she was just waiting longingly to see what I would say. After a few prayerful moments, I said the only thing that came into my mind. "Jesus loves you."

That was it. Three simple words. I didn't read a scripture or recite a prayer. I just said, "Jesus loves you." But the next thing we knew, the old woman forcefully threw off her blankets and stood up! Turning to her husband, she began signing frantically, her hands moving a mile a minute.

Her husband's jaw hung agape, looking at her as if he were seeing a ghost. Shaking his head to snap himself back to reality, he tried to absorb all she was telling him. He then turned from his wife to us, his face still bearing shock and disbelief. "I have never seen her like this before," he said, his voice becoming slowly more exuberant. "She is so happy!" he beamed.

Then he translated her signing for us, "She says she wants you to stay. She wants to cook some spaghetti for all of us to eat!" We all laughed at her response in the wake of this miraculous moment and the early morning hour. We arrived at dawn, and yet she was making spaghetti for us instead of bacon and eggs. She had been completely healed, and like Peter's mother-in-law, the first thing she did was to begin serving us. How funny it was, and I still had not met her son.

Uncle Joe and I followed the man and his wife into the kitchen, watching as she ran about, back and forth, preparing food. Her liveliness dumbfounded us all, but none as much as her husband. I'm sure he couldn't believe this was the same woman who had been lying in pain on the couch just moments ago.

At one point, she paused from her cooking and preparations to come over to me. She opened her arms wide and enveloped me in a bear hug. Uncle Joe smiled and said, "I think she's better!" I just smiled back at him.

After walking into the kitchen I finally set eyes on the young man I had come to meet. I approached him in the midst of the rattling and banging of pots and pans. To my surprise, he looked at me, smiled, and said, "I know why you're here." His smile was genuine, and his demeanor was unexpectedly calm. This wasn't at all what I had imagined. With a confident joy, he proclaimed, "I've already turned my life over to Christ, right before I left prison."

How about that? This young man didn't need me at all! He had already discovered Christ. In fact, he had encountered and been won over by Christ in prison. And so I learned that the Lord hadn't brought me here at all for the purpose of the son. Rather, it was the young man's mother who needed the Lord's healing love. She was the one who was ill and afraid, and God wanted to set her free. It was in fact she who was living in a prison of fear, darkness, and pain.

When our prayer group met next, I shared this story with them, and one of the leaders said something very wise, "It's often not what we do," he said. "We just have to show up, and let God do the rest."

His words were simple, yet profound, and another important lesson learned from the Lord as I walked in his grace. All he asked and required of me was to show up and trust in him. He did the rest. If he asked me to show up, and I did, then surely he would show up as well, and he would not be outdone in generosity. For when he shows up, you better believe that mountains are going to move!

FOURTEEN

Jim & Denise

The vice president of a local hospital called me with the exciting news that he wanted me to put together the hospital's new orientation video! How fortuitous that my good friend Billy had just given me a referral for a very talented young videographer named Jim, and I decided he would be perfect for this hospital project.

Speaking with Jim for the first time, I could tell he was very interested in the job, a sentiment he quickly confirmed by driving to my office. He shook my hand firmly and smiled warmly as I ushered him into the conference room.

We sat down opposite one another and engaged in small talk before getting down to business. As we watched his demo reel and talked about the upcoming project, something very powerful happened to me.

Right there in the conference room, as Jim continued explaining what he could contribute to the project, God interrupted me. I can only describe this particular revelation as an experience akin to watching a movie in my mind about this man's life. Jim's lips continued to move, amidst hand gestures of explanation, but all I could clearly see and hear were these visions of his life, particularly in regards to his wife.

I was like a fly on the wall during some of their most personal communications about having a baby or continuing to pursue their careers. I was also given the knowledge from God in those moments to clearly decipher the situations presented me.

When Jim, at last, finished his demo video and focused his full attention on me, I suddenly felt embarrassed by the fact that I knew him more intimately than I had only a short minute ago. Unbeknownst to him, God had shared the depth of concerns weighing on his heart. Jim certainly wouldn't have shared these of his own accord, especially not during our first encounter. Staring back at me from across the table, Jim still believed we were only connected through a potential business partnership.

"Jim, has anyone ever given you a word of knowledge or prophetic sense from God?" I began. This certainly wasn't the response he was expecting at the close of his marketing presentation."

Well, I'm aware of it," he answered. "Why?"

Embarking on the unknown I said, "Hold onto the conference table Jim because I am about to share an epic revelation."

With that I began. "Jim, God wants to bless you and your wife with a child," I said point blank. That was the first bombshell, and by the look on Jim's face, it was received accordingly. I went on, "He told me that although you and Denise have been trying to conceive, you're not having success." Jim just listened as I continued. "He said that you've been telling her you want a child, but deep inside you are afraid of how a baby could affect your careers and future. I know that your wife is very involved in her career as a camera spokesperson and aspiring singer, but God said he wants you and Denise to prepare for a baby," I said as plainly as I could.

Pausing a moment to allow Jim to fully receive and digest this incredible message from a virtual stranger, I tried to catch his gaze. He stared straight ahead, blankly, as he sat trying to put it all together in his mind. He didn't move a muscle or make a sound. From where I sat, it was an exciting message to deliver from God, but I knew how earth shattering it must have been for him. This message was not an abstract one. In fact, God had given me specific instructions to relay.

"Jim, God told me specifically that he wants you to leave your business, put your house up for sale, and move near your wife's family. She will need this extra support when the baby comes," I instructed. "When you have done this, you will find a new job. You can move in with her family until you find a new house," I affirmed.

"Next, and most importantly, God wants the two of you to visit an obstetrician, because Denise is going to get pregnant soon," I concluded. I knew that for Jim and Denise to follow all I had relayed would take an extreme leap of faith. The last piece of information, however, would surely be the hardest, because Denise believed she couldn't conceive.

"That's it," I said shrugging. "I only offer these words to you, Jim, and I trust you will do with them what is best for you and your wife."

Jim remained staring at me like a deer frozen in the headlights. "Please, Jim," I said gently. "I don't say this to upset you, just think it over."

After a few moments of thoughtful silence, Jim looked directly at me and said, "I don't know how to explain this, but something seems very right about what you are saying. God has just spoken to me through you, revealing many things I have brought before him." I was relieved by the smile that crept across Jim's face. "I have been trying to convince myself of so many lies," he said before boldly stating, "I believe this is God."

And so it was with Jim and me on our first meeting. Shortly after sharing God's words with him, Jim left the office and went home to share the revelation with his wife.

As the weeks passed, I couldn't help but wonder how Denise had reacted to Jim's recounting of all that had transpired in the conference room that day. I was curious and yet fearful to know if Jim would follow the instructions of the Lord, given through me. I was anxious to learn how the rest of this story would unfold.

When Jim and I spoke again about the hospital project, Jim reaffirmed that he believed my words were truly from God. Sometime later, I also found out that Jim had contacted our mutual friend Billy, who had referred me to Jim in the first place. Knowing that Billy was an active Christian, Jim asked him out of the blue, "Have you ever met someone who seems to have a truly prophetic gift?" To this, Billy quickly replied, "Charles Piccirilli." Billy's words were not only confirmation, but they also gave Jim an even deeper comfort in following the radical instructions given to him.

Jim remained in Maryland while we completed the video production, offering me the opportunity to meet Denise as well. We even used her for the project as the on-camera spokesperson. Outwardly, the three of us kept our focus on the professional production, but Jim was slowly making changes in his personal life. He and Denise put their house up for sale and began making plans to move nearer her parents in Virginia Beach.

We finished the video and played it for my client, who was very pleased. When he presented it to the president of the hospital, the president not only gave it high praise, but offered a very strange response as well. He said, "Do you notice anything unusual about this video?" Jim and I exchanged an unknowing glance. "It looks like God himself was directing it," he said oddly. To this day I'm not quite sure exactly what he meant by that, but for Jim it was certainly another confirmation. There was no doubt that Jim and Denise were concretely experiencing God's direction in their lives.

With the project completed, Jim left his company and moved to Virginia Beach with his wife. There he began looking for a new job. And as they did, in fact, begin to take these concrete steps according to the prophecy, I was attacked again and again by a spirit of doubt.

I became overwhelmed with thoughts that I was a fool.
"Why would God speak to me?" the voice chastised. "Who am
I? What if I have just contributed to a series of disastrous life
changes for Jim and Denise?" the voice accused, always in the
first person.

Yet I knew that Jim was faithfully following a word of knowledge
from the Lord, and this meant big changes as well as sacrifices.
He was stepping out in blind faith, based on my message. What if
I was wrong?

But I could not allow myself to be consumed by these doubts.
I had to trust God and the message he gave to me for Jim and
Denise, regardless of the constant attacks. In these moments,
I remembered the Lord's words to Jacob in Isaiah 41:9-10,
"You are my servant, I have chosen you and not cast you off;
fear not, for I am with you."

Thankfully, Jim put me out of my misery, calling several weeks
later to report that he had gotten a wonderful position at a large
production company. He sounded happy about the position,
but all was not going as smoothly throughout their transition.
Their house in Maryland was not selling, and things were getting
tight financially with them paying for both an apartment and a
mortgage. God definitely was stretching their faith at this point,
as well as my own.

As it turned out, the vice president of the hospital was so
impressed with our work that he again gave me a commission.
This time, he wanted us to create a television commercial for the
hospital's retirement home. This great opportunity could not have
come at a better time, and I was looking forward to visiting Jim
and Denise as much as working with them on another project.
Shortly after Jim and I planned the trip, I packed my car and
headed down to Virginia Beach.

It was a happy reunion as Jim and I anxiously shared with one
another our ideas for the new project! He also was able to show

me around the new studio where he was working. We would be filming the commercial at this location, in a space he was leasing for his own personal business. After adequately assessing the studio setup and drawing up plans for the coming weeks, we decided to meet Denise for dinner.

The food at the seafood restaurant they chose was magnificent, and at first, the mood at our table seemed to be one of happy re-acquaintance. However, as our meal continued, Denise grew more and more somber. I could tell she was unhappy, and it became clear she was not as excited by my visit as her husband was.

After moving some food around carefully on her plate for some time, she finally looked up and said, "Charles, I have to tell you that I am hurting, discouraged, and desperately trying to hold onto the belief that God is going to give me a child, but it's not easy." There was a sting in her voice that pained me as she continued, "We have listened to you, but I have been told that it is medically impossible for me to conceive."

My appetite began to quickly diminish as Denise's strong emotion moved both Jim and me with concern. In a voice filled with worry, she went on, "I also have a friend my age that is pregnant, and she was told by her doctor that the child in her womb will be born with physical defects." In utter defeat, Denise's sad gaze was cast downward toward her plate once again. In a barely audible voice, she concluded, "Our house in Maryland still hasn't sold, and we can't afford having two monthly payments. What more are we supposed to do, Charles?"

My stomach churned as her words brought back the previous doubts that had haunted me. I sank deeply into my chair and bowed my head. There was nothing else to do at this point except to turn to God. I called on him from within my heart in that moment, pleading with him to help me, to tell me what to do. I was heartbroken that things didn't seem to be turning out as I had conveyed. In quiet desperation, I listened for God, wondering what to do now.

Faithfully he interrupted my thoughts and again gave me an answer. He firmly whispered into my heart, and as he did, all doubt and despair dissipated. He was still there, still in control of this situation, and I could be assured that what he had said was true. I lifted my head to Jim and Denise, who were both staring at me.

"God just told me that you did not go to the obstetrician as he had instructed you to do."

Jim quickly looked to his wife and said, "He's right! We followed everything he said to do, except that. I left my company, put the house up for sale, moved to Virginia Beach to be near your parents, and found a new job. But, we didn't make an appointment with an obstetrician. Denise, we need to do that right away." Jim's fervor made my heart jump, and I was renewed with peace. After finishing our meal, I made the long trip back to Maryland, praying all the way home.

Three months after our dinner at that seafood restaurant, the phone on my office desk rang at about 10:30 a.m. Jim's voice greeted me on the other end with an excitement that couldn't be contained. "Hi, Charles. this is Jim" he almost giggled. "I am calling because Denise and I want you to be the very first to hear this," he continued, almost giddy now. "We went to the obstetrician after your visit. Denise had some testing done, which determined that she wasn't ovulating. She was given a medication to help her ovulate, and two months later, we learned that Denise is pregnant!"

Jim was ecstatic and smiling through the phone. "It's a miracle, Charles! You were right about the obstetrician being the missing piece of the puzzle. Denise is pregnant!" My heart jumped inside my chest at the news. He went on, "We also got a call from our realtor telling us our house in Maryland sold!" Almost bubbling over now, he said, "Bless you, Charles, for being faithful to God."

It was that blessing, which was truly the greatest gift from Jim and from God. At that moment, there was rejoicing throughout my entire being. God had been faithful to me as well as to Jim and Denise. He had done what he said he would do. It fell upon me only to be faithful in delivering the message, and it fell upon Jim to be faithful in following it.

Looking back, I can't say that doubt never crept into my heart along the way, and doubt certainly haunted Denise. Yet through it all, Jim persevered in his conviction that my words were truly from God, and he was certain that these words would be fulfilled.

Nine months later, Jim and Denise's first daughter Tess Ann was born, followed years later by her sister Cassie Lee, and finally their son Jonathan. Praise God for his gift of knowledge and faith, but most of all for the gift of children, given to his servants, Jim and Denise.

"He gives the barren woman a home, making her the joyous mother of children. Praise the Lord!" (Psalm 113:9)

FIFTEEN

The Gift of Understanding

One of the ways the Lord has chosen to reveal himself to me is through the parables of scripture. There are times when I not only read the parables, but I also experience them very personally. Here are two such examples of how the parables of scripture came alive for me

The Parable of the Sower (Matthew 13:1-23)

In the parable of the sower, Jesus tells the crowds, *"A sower went out to sow. And as he sowed, some seeds fell along the path, and the birds came and devoured them."*

Jesus explains to his disciples the meaning of this parable, *"When anyone hears the word of the kingdom and does not understand it, the evil one comes and snatches away what is sown in his heart; this is what was sown along the path."* I shudder when I think of the power of truth in that testimony, witnessing to the spiritual gift of understanding. Without it, the word of God is in danger, even within our own hearts.

The disciples ask Jesus why he uses parables to teach the crowds. To this Jesus tells them they have been given a special knowledge of the secrets of heaven, which the people hearing the parables have not. The crowds can better understand his messages through parables. Jesus recalls the prophecy in Isaiah 6, which promises a remnant of faithful believers. The disciples are these promised faithful remnant foretold by Isaiah. They will spread the message after Christ is gone.

Again, God shoots straight from the hip concerning all matters of sin, yet always giving us hope.

The people only have to turn to the Lord and ask for his healing, his help, and his guidance, but instead, they turn away. They choose the harder paths that lead to destruction, and they even become blind to the magnitude of the choices before them.

Jesus answers the disciples in Matthew 13:14-15 by showing them how this prophecy is fulfilled in the people of the crowds before them:

> *"You shall indeed hear but never understand, and you shall indeed see but never perceive. For this people's heart has grown dull, and their ears are heavy of hearing, and their eyes they have closed, lest they should perceive with their eyes, and hear with their ears, and understand with their heart, and turn for me to heal them.'"*

"Wow Lord!" I thought when I read these verses. "Please let me hear and understand, as well as spiritually perceive what I am seeing. Please don't let my heart grow dull, my ears grow heavy, or my eyes close," I fervently prayed. "Please Lord, whatever I need, give it to me. Give me understanding."

The Parable Explained to Me

It didn't take the Lord long to oblige. As the Holy Spirit began to reveal this teaching of Jesus to me clearly in a unique way, I was especially moved by an event after one of our Friday night prayer meetings. My young sons, Micah and Joshua, followed Mary and me out of the prayer meeting, each carrying a paper cup filled with dirt. Stuffed down deep in the dirt of each cup was a small pumpkin seed.

As we drove home, they bubbled over from the back seat about all they had learned about the birds on the path in Matthew's parable. Excitedly, they explained how they had to guard their pumpkin seeds just like the seeds of their faith. All the while they were clutching their small cups closer to their chests. Mary and I shared a smile, knowing that our young sons were learning about the Lord.

When we arrived home, Micah asked if they could keep their little cups in their bedroom so that they could watch over them. I could just imagine Mary's reaction to having muddy little cups invading her spotless home.

"Mommy would be very upset about having them in the house," I said, "but you can put them on top of the picnic table where they will be nice and safe. You can get them first thing in the morning." That seemed to be a fair compromise for the boys, who followed me out to the table where they carefully placed their little cups.

As I was preparing my coffee the next morning, I looked out the window, remembering the cups. When I saw them lying on their sides, I ran out to put them upright before the boys noticed.

Assuming the wind blew them over during the night, when I picked up the little cups, to my surprise, I saw that the seeds were gone!

I then realized that birds must have stolen the precious seeds right out of the cups, just like the birds did in the parable. And in that instant, the parable became real to me. I understood. The Lord not only wanted me to hear his words, but he also needed me to understand them so they could take root in my heart. With that, the Lord told me to stand firmly behind his teachings concerning my own family, and particularly that of my sons.

The Parable of the Barren Fig Tree (Luke 13:6-9)

I think many of us take comfort in the vinedresser's dedication to the little barren fig tree in the parable. Perhaps it's out of his own pride, fear of failure, or fear of disappointing the owner of the fig tree that the vinedresser begs him to leave the tree alone for just one more year. In that time, he will give the tree special attention to help it bear fruit.

And he told this parable.

> *"A man had a fig tree planted in his vineyard; and he came seeking fruit on it and found none. And he said to the vinedresser, 'Lo, these three years I have come seeking fruit on this fig tree, and I find none. Cut it down; why should it use up the ground?' And he answered him, 'Let it alone, sir, this year also, till I dig about it and put on manure. And if it bears fruit next year, well and good; but if not, you can cut it down.'"*

The Parable Explained by Me

Every summer I would plant tomatoes in a three by thirty-foot patch of ground behind our row house. Two of my neighbors did likewise.

One summer, as the three of us stood around our patches planning our annual tomato crop, I challenged them to a tomato race. "Let's see who gets the first tomatoes!" I taunted as I began to turn my soil.

They eagerly agreed, and the three of us began planting our small crops at the same time and tending them daily, in hopes of achieving those coveted bragging rights.

I had to laugh at their enthusiasm over the contest. One of the neighbors, a young Polish girl, had garden soil that was as hard as clay. The other neighbor, an elderly man who lived across the alley, had very rich soil, which he often fed and maintained. My soil was decent, somewhere in between that of my two neighbors.

I was very satisfied as I watched my plants rise to about two feet tall and begin budding a few small yellow flowers. Across the alley, I could see that the mounds of Miracle Grow and manure my elderly neighbor heaped around his small plants had produced leafy green structures that stood almost four feet high.

Not surprisingly, our young Polish neighbor's plants were less impressive, standing only about a foot high. Despite their diminutive stature, however, her plants already were yielding little tomatoes. "How in the world were her plants getting tomatoes already?" I wondered. "And even with that awful soil!" As I stood there baffled, I felt the Lord nudging me, and I knew he was trying to teach me something through this little example.

I decided to do some research, so I drove to the Agricultural Extension Service in Harford County, hoping for an explanation for this phenomenon. I described the neighborly competition and the three types of soil and treatment we each had administered to our crops. I asked how it was possible for the smallest plants in the least desirable soil to bear fruit, while our lofty plants in superior soil had not.

The agriculturists were not at all baffled by this mystery. They agreed that my soil was average, and my plants reflected an average growth. My elderly neighbor's soil was too rich, and therefore it was not producing any flowers. The girl's plants, on the other hand, somehow knew they were planted in bad soil, which ultimately kept them under constant stress.

"Isn't that a bad thing?" I asked.

"You would think," they replied. "The girl's plants know they are dying, therefore they are trying to bear as much fruit as possible before the end." Then they advised me to go home and take a knife to my plants. They said to kill some of the roots around them, but to take care not to cut too much.

It seemed counterintuitive to me to take a knife to my plant's roots, knowingly putting them in distress. Nonetheless, I went home and did as I was told. To my great surprise, a few days later, my plants began to bear tomatoes as well! This was a significant lesson to me from the Lord. As I reflected on the parable of the fig tree, the Lord explained that the cares of this world were keeping me from bearing the fruit required of me. He was calling me to die to myself and rise in him, through obedience to his will.

All at once I was able to see it clearly; suffering is a gift. When we suffer in Christ, we produce fruit for his kingdom and learn to rejoice in it. In all my years since this lesson, when asked to suffer, I am reminded of those tomato plants. I ask that through my suffering I might experience his grace and bear fruit.

> *"More than that, we rejoice in our sufferings, knowing that suffering produces endurance, and endurance produces character, and character produces hope, and hope does not disappoint us because God's love has been poured into our hearts through the Holy Spirit who has been given to us." (Romans 5:3-6)*

The gifts of the Holy Spirit sustain and strengthen our moral life, bearing fruit within us, coming to full maturation in eternal glory. We should ask for the gift of understanding, which was lacking in the people to whom Isaiah prophesied, as well as the crowds to which Jesus told parables. The gift of understanding continues to be slowly and simply revealed to me, sometimes even through ordinary things such as tomato plants and pumpkin seeds! Let us see in all things the glory of God.

SIXTEEN

The Cause of the Bleed

I have always taken joy in my nephew Chris and his wife Beth, who are a lovely example of a young Catholic couple. That is why I was particularly distressed one evening when we found out Beth started to experience a horrible pain in her head that was accompanied by sudden illness. Chris described how Beth had become ill so quickly that she began losing consciousness. He immediately had called for an ambulance, and Beth was rushed to the hospital.

When they arrived, the doctor caring for Beth said her situation was gravely serious. It seemed that she was suffering from an aneurysm or brain tumor. Either way, the prognosis wasn't good, and there was low expectancy of survival.

Mary and I, having a special place in our hearts for Chris and Beth, were tremendously upset by this news. Despite our awareness of the fragility of life, it was still hard to fathom a terminal illness coming on so quickly to such a beautiful and healthy young girl who was so full of life.

I was overcome with a strong sense that I was needed at the hospital. God assured me that once I was there, he would reveal what I was to do and pray for in this situation.

Mary was by my side once again as we walked into the hospital. We weren't sure what to expect, or even if we'd be allowed into Beth's room, but again I knew that I needed to follow the Lord on this one.

When we arrived, we met Beth and Chris' parents in the waiting room. Beth's mother was distraught and sadly said to us, *"This is not going well. This is not going to have a happy outcome."* Her heart was aching, and she was trying her best to prepare for what seemed to be the inevitable.

I had no words for Beth's mother at the time. All I knew was that I needed to get to Beth and physically lay my hands on her to pray. The Lord had put this much of his plan before me, and I knew he soon would reveal the rest clearly.

I waited surreptitiously for a hurried nurse or doctor to swing open the doors of the intensive care unit, which allowed me to slip through cautiously and make my way down the hallway. I was on a mission, and as I turned the corner into Beth's room and saw her lying there, I lovingly greeted her with a smile and rested my hands upon her.

As soon as I did this, the Lord began to speak. His words were clear and direct, and perhaps the last thing I expected to hear. *"This is not an aneurysm or a tumor,"* he said. *"It is a bleed, as a consequence of using artificial contraception."* Taken aback, I just listened. *"Her body has already begun to absorb this bleed."*

As Beth lay there motionless on the hospital bed, already paralyzed on one side of her body, the Lord spoke further, *"Her paralysis will quickly begin to leave her. She will recover fully."* As the Lord reassured me that Beth would have a full recovery, I was totally overcome with joy and gladness. My eyes filled with warm tears, as I showered the Lord with words of praise and thanksgiving.

I left the room and made my way back to our frazzled and worried party in the waiting room. The joy and relief they saw on my face undoubtedly surprised Chris and his parents. I excitedly shared with them the Lord's revelation and assurance of her full recovery. My brother-in-law looked kindly at me saying, "Thank you, Brother." It was not the first time he had witnessed the Lord's intervention, but this would be a new experience for Beth's parents.

I approached them nonetheless and attempted to comfort them as well with the Lord's promise of their daughter's healing. As you can imagine, they were resistant to accepting any assurance from me or even from the medical staff.

Mary and I returned home and when the phone rang the next day, I answered it and heard the smooth and calm voice of my brother-in-law Bob. "Brother," he said, "we have a miracle!"

After being transferred to another hospital, the doctors discovered that Beth had not suffered an aneurysm or brain tumor. She had suffered a brain bleed, and her body had already absorbed the bleed. Her paralysis also had been temporary. Thankfully, Beth experienced a full recovery and quickly returned to her happy and healthy life.

I thanked the Lord for healing her and for allowing me to participate. I never told any of them about the revelation that oral contraception was the cause of the bleed. But I would be remiss if I didn't ask the Lord why he allowed this to happen, "What lesson are you sharing?"

After ten years, I finally decided to call Beth and recount the story, giving her the exact details. I asked her to reveal the medical diagnosis of her brain bleed. For the first time in ten years, it was confirmed to me that the medical findings attributed the bleed to Beth's use of artificial hormonal contraception.

I was again reminded of my own use of artificial contraception in my marriage, and how it had poisoned my two unborn sons, who are now in heaven. I was so thankful that the Lord intervened for Beth before it took her life.

Not even a year later, Aaron, my youngest son called me on the phone. His voice was somber as he said, "Dad, will you come to the hospital and pray for my friend Josh and his wife Amy? She's just had a major stroke." Without thinking, I knew right away what was wrong with Amy. "I'm on my way," I said to Aaron, and I sped off to meet him.

As we entered Amy's hospital room, I couldn't get over how much she resembled Beth in this similar state. I sat beside Amy's hospital bed, and again the Lord revealed to me that her symptoms also resulted from the use of artificial contraception.

I took her hand in mine and directly asked, "Amy, are you and Josh on the pill?"

Stunned, she looked at me strangely before mumbling, "Yes."

With tenderness and comfort, still holding her hand in mine, I said, "You're going to be okay. You have a brain bleed due to the use of oral contraception, but you will recover."

Aaron and Josh looked at me, astonished that I could know what the doctors did not yet know. I looked at my son and said, "I knew before we even arrived. God was using me again to share the truth about the dangers of artificial contraception."I also told Josh directly that they needed to stop taking the pill. Amy quickly recovered and was released from the hospital and from her illness as well.

For a third time, the Lord allowed this same incident to occur. Someone very close to me was in the hospital with quite different symptoms altogether. And yet when I sat beside her hospital bed, it was revealed that her illness was also due to artificial contraception. She and her husband were surprised and embarrassed that I could know of the use of something so personal and saddened that it may have led to her current medical state. Thankfully, she also recovered.

The evils of artificial contraception use were starkly before me. They were divinely presented three distinct times in very explicit ways, beyond the revelation of my own contraceptive use in marriage. In reflecting on this revelation, it was clearly put on my heart to share these dangers with others—not only the physical complications I had witnessed, but also a lurking evil that was much more deadly.

I decided to reach out to Father Michael DeAscanis, who was pastor of St. William of York Church in Southwest Baltimore. After I explained my desire to offer Natural Family Planning as a viable option for couples seeking an alternative to artificial contraception, Father Michael was not only enthusiastically supportive, but he also was adamant that I hold a conference right there at St. William of York.

He strongly felt this was especially significant because on August 4, 1968, in the basement of St. William of York's rectory, a large group of priests had gathered to discuss the encyclical letter, *Humanae Vitae*. The discussion was not favorable toward the teaching of the Holy Father, and it ultimately resulted in the priests signing their names to the Washington statement of dissent. The blatant disobedience of so many priests haunted the Church for years, and Father Michael saw this as a perfect opportunity to reverse what had been done there.

So, on Saturday, September 15, 2012, I held a conference at St. William of York called "Planning for Life." It was meant to give hope to those seeking an alternative to the physically and spiritually unhealthy use of artificial contraception. It particularly shed light on the healthy, safe, and scientifically advanced alternative in Christ.

Doctors, priests, counselors, and married couples climbed the stage to speak on the day of the conference. They shared research, advice, and personal messages about their journeys and discoveries of the use of natural methods as opposed to the use of artificial contraception. The divisive evil residing in the seemingly innocent marital practice of contraceptive was overwhelming.

At last, the powerful truth of the prophetic message delivered over forty years ago in *Humanae Vitae* was confirmed for many that day, and continues to be revealed today.

Consequences of Artificial Methods of Contraception from the encyclical letter, *Humanae Vitae*

"Responsible men can become more deeply convinced of the truth of the doctrine laid down by the Church on this issue if they reflect on the consequences of methods and plans for artificial birth control. Let them first consider how easily this course of action could open wide the way for marital infidelity and a general lowering of moral standards. Not much experience is needed to be fully aware of human weakness and to understand that human beings–and especially the young, who are so exposed to temptation–need incentives to keep the moral law, and it is an evil thing to make it easy for them to break that law. Another effect that gives cause for alarm is that a man who grows accustomed to the use of contraceptive methods may forget the reverence due to a woman, and, disregarding her physical and emotional equilibrium, reduce her to being a mere instrument for the satisfaction of his own desires, no longer considering her as his partner whom he should surround with care and affection.

"Finally, careful consideration should be given to the danger of this power passing into the hands of those public authorities who care little for the precepts of the moral law. Who will blame a government which in its attempt to resolve the problems affecting an entire country resorts to the same measures as are regarded as lawful by married people in the solution of a particular family difficulty? Who will prevent public authorities from favoring those contraceptive methods, which they consider more effective? Should they regard this as necessary, they may even impose their use on everyone. It could well happen, therefore, that when people, either individually or in family or social life, experience the inherent difficulties of the divine law and are determined to avoid them, they may give into the hands of public authorities the power to intervene in the most personal and intimate responsibility of husband and wife."

(Encyclical Letter Humanae Vitae of the Supreme Pontiff Paul VI, July 25, 1968)

SEVENTEEN

Spiritual Comfort on a Cruise

When our dear friends Wayne and Maria invited Mary and me to join them and our friend Howard on a cruise, we jumped at the opportunity. Excitedly, we began packing our bags and thought about the warm sunny days and peaceful ocean breezes ahead. On this cruise, however, I would learn that God is part of our vacation as much as he is part of our daily life. God is with us always, and he allows us to participate in his glory, even in the most unexpected places.

Boarding the ship with the other smiling and chatty passengers, Mary and I made our way to our cabin. The journey started as you might expect. We shared the wonderful company of our friends in cheerful laughter around the pool and at the dinner table, while also enjoying other entertaining and relaxing activities.

One day after a beautiful shore excursion, I remember how excited I was to board the ship again. They were serving my all-time favorite food for dinner…lobster! Oh, how I love lobster! It was all I could think about that day. Just before dinner, Mary went for a swim, while Wayne and I went to the front of the ship to watch the sun set over the ocean. It seemed to be the perfect end to our day.

As we gazed out over the glassy sea below, I noticed small ripples traveling across the water just behind the ship. "Look at those little waves," I remarked.

Wayne, who was an ex-navy man, looked at me in surprise and replied, "Those are not little ripples. I bet they are more than eight feet tall." Looking down from our very high vantage point, everything seemed small. Those "little" ripples began to increase rapidly, however, and I noticed that the large ship began rocking.

I walked around the deck to the back of the ship and found Mary helping a little boy out of the pool and onto the deck before jumping out herself. "Did you see that?" she demanded, as I helped her gather her things. "We could have drowned!" The water had become disturbingly turbulent by then. In fact, the boat was rocking to the point of causing water to wash out of the swimming pool and across the deck, and then sending it rushing back in again.

As the water got even rougher, and the boat began to sway, all passengers went below deck. An announcement from the captain projected over the loudspeaker warned us of a brief period of roughness as the ship's rudders were being balanced. Mary and I tried to take our minds off the rocking and went to our cabin to dress for dinner. We talked nervously about our day as we headed up to the restaurant to meet our friends.

Despite the lure of lobster, the closer we got to the dining room, with the rocking of the ship, the less I felt like eating. I was feeling too ill to think about food, even if it was lobster. I told Mary I needed some air, and we headed back above deck so I could lie down on one of the ship's lounge chairs. Yet lying there, gazing over the deep moving darkness, didn't seem to help at all. Amidst the damp air was nothing more than a growing sense of nausea.

Still, by my side, Mary finally felt that I needed medical attention. There was an infirmary on the lower deck, so the two of us hobbled along to the safe shelter of the nearest elevator. I began asking the Lord, "Why are you letting this happen to me?" I knew by now that he always had a plan, but did that plan have to be on lobster night?

Yes, of course it did! He had certainly gotten my attention.
So once again, I submitted all to him, saying, "I know you are
in full control Lord. You are in control of the wind and seas, and
even of how I am feeling right now. You could stop any of it in
an instant if you decided to. Either way, I thank you Lord, and I
praise you for your love."

As soon as the elevator doors opened on the lower deck,
I suddenly was no longer sick. Just like that, it was gone!
I looked over at Mary, who had been doing her best to support
my weight with her tiny frame. "Well, the sickness is gone,"
I said matter-of-factly. "We can go back up to dinner!"

I could have sworn by the look on her face that Mary was ready
to make me worthy of the infirmary herself. She guided me out
of the open elevator door and insisted that I might as well get a
shot for my motion sickness since we were already there. So, in
we went.

We sat down in the small waiting area of the ship's infirmary
across from a young lady who held a pair of men's shoes in her
lap. I smiled at her and asked why she was there. She calmly
responded that her husband had gotten sick to his stomach, and
the doctor was with him. I assumed he must have had a touch of
the same motion sickness that had hit me, and I hoped it would
pass just as quickly for him. But as I sat and waited, looking
around the room, God interrupted my thoughts. "Her husband
has died," he said.

Shocked by what I had just heard the Lord say to me, I turned to
Mary and quietly whispered into her ear. She looked at me and
then at the woman, asking if I was sure. After sitting there quietly
for about ten minutes, the Captain came into the waiting area
with us and locked the door behind him. In the midst of all the
commotion, Mary and I watched as the Lord's grievous message
began to be revealed.

Suddenly there was a knock at the door, and the young woman's brother-in-law and sister-in-law were led into the room with us. All the while, the young woman just sat there quietly, holding her husband's shoes in her lap. Her brother-in-law joined the doctor for a few moments in the back. When he returned to the waiting area, he gently knelt beside the young woman and told her that her husband had passed away.

Her face melted into a mass of hysterical tears, and the three of them sat huddled together, holding one another as they grieved and sobbed. My heart ached for them, and it was at that moment that the Holy Spirit moved me to say something.

I saw now why the Lord had brought me to the infirmary at this exact moment. He placed a verse on my heart, which he wanted me to share as a way to comfort the wife, brother, and sister-in-law of the man who had just died. From the recesses of my body, I found my voice and spoke these words to them, "You know Lazarus, the brother of Mary and Martha was extremely ill." Everyone in the room looked up at me in surprise, and I began to recount the story for them.

> "Mary and Martha immediately sent word to Jesus that the one he loved very much was sick. Jesus then said, 'This illness is not unto death; it is for the glory of God, so that the Son of God may be glorified by means of it.' Jesus loved the three of them very much, but stayed two more days before saying, 'Let us go into Judea again.' Despite the danger awaiting him there, he insisted, 'Our friend Lazarus has fallen asleep, but I go to awake him out of sleep.' His disciples replied, 'Lord, if he has fallen asleep, he will recover.' Jesus had been speaking of Lazarus' death, but his disciples thought he meant natural sleep. Jesus then told them plainly, 'Lazarus is dead; and for your sake, I am glad that I was not there, so that you may believe. But let us go to him.'"

The young woman holding her husband's shoes suddenly became peaceful and somewhat accepting as I continued recounting the words from John's Gospel. All three of them listened quietly and intently.

> "'Lord, if you had been here, my brother would not have died. And even now I know that whatever you ask from God, God will give you.' Jesus said to her, 'Your brother will rise again.' Martha answered, 'I know that he will rise again in the resurrection at the last day.' Then Jesus said to her, 'I am the resurrection and the life; he who believes in me, though he die, yet shall he live, and whoever lives and believes in me shall never die, forever. Do you believe this?'"

The ship's infirmary waiting room was silent as I finished recounting the powerful story of Lazarus. I didn't even know if the woman and her family were Christian, but I asked them just the same— "Do you believe this is true?" After several affirmative nods, Mary and I joined hands with them, and we prayed together right then and there, in the ship's small infirmary waiting room. I lifted my voice to the Lord like never before, asking him to bring peace and joy to this family.

When the medical team finally unlocked the doors of the small room and informed us that we were free to leave, Mary and I hugged the grieving family and quietly entered the elevator. As it took us higher and farther from the infirmary, we looked at one another and were overwhelmed by the continuous working hand of God in our lives. Overcome by emotion, I could only say, "Isn't it amazing that God can use us to share the good news of Jesus with those in need?" We were sad for their loss but blessed that the Lord had given us that moment to share in their sadness and offer them his consolation.

When we arrived at the restaurant, Mary and I were surprised to find our friends still there waiting for us, wondering why we were so late. There on the table in front of us were two lobster dinners!

Mary and I sat with our friends, savoring every delicious bite of lobster while sharing with them what had just transpired below deck.

The next day, several people told me that a young woman was looking everywhere for the preacher who had helped her handle the news of her husband's passing the day before. Oh, boy! I was certainly no preacher, just an eager disciple of the Lord. When she found me, she thanked me profusely for sharing my love with them.

To be honest, I hadn't known what to say at all in those moments in the infirmary. I realized that the only compassion and love I had to share with her was given through Christ, whose love is abundantly overflowing and always desiring to be shared. That love was more than enough!

EIGHTEEN

Consequences for Sin

It was almost lunchtime on a bright August day, and I had about fifteen dollars in my pocket. I could no longer resist the temptation to take a walk outside and enjoy the fresh air. Sliding my chair out from behind my desk, with a nice big salad on my mind, I left the office and crossed the street to Klein's Supermarket.

I grabbed a disposable bowl and began to load up on greens, artichoke hearts, different varieties of olive salads, and hard-boiled pickled eggs. I piled one thing right on top of the other. My mouth was watering as I presented my hefty bowl to the girl behind the register.

Just in front of the register was a small rotisserie oven with golden-brown Cornish hens rotating slowly over a flame. They were dripping with juice and the smell as they roasted suddenly made me question my salad choice. Figuring that I had about a five-dollar salad before me, I noticed that the price of a roasted hen was about the same.

"Gee, I could have gotten one of these chickens for five bucks instead of a bowl of greens, huh?" I laughingly remarked to the young girl behind the register.

She smiled in amused agreement, but when she placed my salad on the scale to weigh it, the price was a whopping twelve dollars and ninety-eight cents! I was shocked. "That can't be right," I said.

Sympathetic to my response, she agreed, saying, "You're right. That does seem very expensive. Something must be wrong with the register or the scale. Let me restart everything." After a few resets and calling another cashier to check it as well, the price came up one cent higher! It was now twelve dollars and ninety-nine cents.

By now we were both frustrated, and she decided to help me out. She placed my salad half on the scale and half off, and the price came up to just four dollars and fifty cents. "How's that?" she asked.

With a big smile, I enthusiastically replied, "Great!" I paid the four dollars and fifty cents for my salad, crossed the street to my office building, and sat down to enjoy my lunch. I felt satisfied, just the way you feel when you've made a good deal.

But as I put my fork into the salad, God interrupted me. *"What are you doing?"* he said. I stopped and thought.

"What am I doing, Lord?" I couldn't think of why he was asking this scolding question.

In a moment's time, however, the Lord made it abundantly clear to me. *"You stole that salad,"* he said. *"And even worse than that, you led that young cashier into sin as well."* I looked down at my bowl. How could a salad, of all things, lead someone into sin?

Suddenly my "good deal" didn't seem so impressive. I stopped eating, realizing that the only thing to do was to right the wrong. I had to go back to the supermarket and confess to the owner. I needed to repent for my sin, and in so doing, give him the money back. I could barely finish my lunch, convicted of what I had done wrong and what was now required of me.

I decided to go back the following day and give the owner twenty dollars (the money I owed, plus some), while not revealing the name of the cashier.

The salad was only the beginning of the lesson the Lord was teaching me, however. It was the groundwork, if you will, for a greater education.

You see, as a hobby photographer, I saved up for, and took very good care of, the expensive camera equipment I was able to purchase.

I recently had sent out my Canon XL2 video camera to New York for repair. I was so excited to get it back and begin working with it again. When I called Mary later that day, she confirmed that a box had come in the mail for me. I couldn't wait to get home and see how well my camera worked.

I practically flew through the door of our house, my eyes laser focusing in on the large brown box on the counter. Like a child at Christmas, I grabbed the box and quickly tore it open. To my surprise, all I found inside was one part of my camera. I searched through the crumpled padding in the box, but it was clear that the lens and microphone were missing.

"What could have happened to the rest of my camera?" I thought, exasperated and confused. I picked up the phone right away and called the repair company to straighten it out.

The gentleman who answered the phone checked my repair order and assured me, "That's all you sent."

Shocked by his flippant response and feeling my anger begin to rise, I told the man, "No, I sent you the whole camera." He insisted that the box I sent weighed only three pounds, while the full camera would have weighed nine pounds. After a stalemate conversation, the man agreed to check again with his repairman and get back to me.

I knew that I had sent the entire camera in a box weighing nine pounds. Before I completely lost my temper, I stopped and turned toward the Lord, asking him what he could be teaching me in all of this. Suddenly...I thought of the salad.

Mary looked at me from across the room as I paused in revelation. I told her what had happened earlier that day, and how God had gotten angry with me. I now understood the lesson he was teaching me, now that it came to my own property that had been stolen.

Right then and there I began to thank and praise God for being so tough on me, and for giving me such a quick resolution to repenting for my sin. "Oh Lord, you surely know how to discipline the ones you love," I said.

The next morning, I started on my quest to track down my camera. After I had called the local post office and everywhere in between, a young friend named Dan walked into my office. I began recounting the whole sordid situation to him. As I tied the two incidents of the salad and the camera together, I could tell by his doubtful expression that Dan thought it was quite a stretch.

He laughed as I assuredly concluded that God was loving and teaching me through his rebuke, by allowing my camera to be taken away. It was all part of God's lesson. "I have to go back to Klein's Supermarket and repent to the owner," I told Dan. "I have to give back the money I stole."

Dan told me to slow down before making such a bold connection, which still seemed like a leap to him. Perhaps the two incidents were more appropriately coincidence, or at the very least, the result of an overactive conscience!

"Are you nuts?" he said when I told him I was going to return the money to the manager. "Do you really believe that God reprimanded you for stealing a salad, and then as a consequence, used your camera to drive home the point?"

I really did believe it, and I was confident that returning the money was what I needed to do. So, off to Klein's I went, boldly asking to see the owner.

The tired man came up to me reluctantly, assuming I was there to make a complaint. In quite a serious manner, I confessed to him that I had stolen a salad from his store and asked him if he would forgive me. I placed twenty dollars in his hand, and he stared at for a few long moments while he digested my words.

He then looked up quizzically from his hand to the sincerity on my face before saying matter-of-factly, "Okay, I'll put the money in the register." He didn't ask me to identify the cashier, and I was thankful for that.

Crossing the street back to the office, I felt as if a great weight was lifted from my soul, and I was very happy. Dan was still there when I returned, possibly hanging around to see if I would actually go through with the repentance plan.

When I walked in beaming, he asked me again, "Do you really believe that the salad has something to do with your camera?" Again, I replied, "Of course I do. Can't you see it?"

This was not only a teaching moment for me, but it also was one for my friend Dan. "The Lord loves us, Dan," I said, "and he disciplines those he loves. He disciplines us and shows himself to each of us in very different ways. This is according to our relationship with him, our nature, and the way that we learn best."

I could tell that Dan was being drawn in by what I was saying and that something was resonating with him. "Yes, I can see that God often uses a similar pattern in my life as well," he affirmed.

"Exactly!" I said excitedly. "With me, God always works in a similar way. I can usually tell when he is disciplining me, and yet, following each discipline is a teaching or blessing."

Dan smiled in understanding, and I raised my voice joyfully
as I proclaimed, "Dan, the day isn't over yet. I'm telling you,
the Lord always responds to me!"

When I arrived home that evening, Mary had some great news
to share with me. "Honey," she said excitedly, "I found the
postage receipt for your camera!" I could have jumped right out
of my skin.

And God bless her because I usually lay all my receipts on the
table for her to throw away after she writes them down in the
checkbook. With prudence, however, she usually saves them in
a small box for a time, rather than throwing them out right away.
After searching through the receipts, she found the one from the
post office verifying that I had sent a nine-pound box to
New York.

I grabbed the receipt, waving it around like a golden ticket and
laughing with joy. I began praising God, dancing around the
kitchen like King David had danced before the Ark, telling him
how mighty and great he was.

I picked up the phone directly and called the camera repair center
in New York. When the man answered and I told him about the
receipt confirmation, he answered, "I already know Mr. Piccirilli.
We found the rest of your camera earlier today."

The missing pieces arrived, as good as new, the very next day.
The Lord had answered me, just as I said he would. There was
only one more thing to do—I had to call Dan and confirm God's
blessing following his lesson.

When I heard his voice on the other end of the line, I just said,
"Dan, God loves me!" He laughed surprisingly, not ready to
believe what he was about to hear. I recounted how Mary found
the missing receipt and the repair center found and sent the
camera parts—and it all had happened before the day was over!

After a few moments, Dan just said, "Amen."

When I tell people these stories of God's discipline and blessings in my life, they usually respond by saying, "This kind of stuff only happens to you." But it's not only me. It can't be only me because this promise is for all of us.

In 2 Chronicles 7:14, God says, *"If my people who are called by my name humble themselves, and pray and seek my face, and turn from their wicked ways, then I will hear from heaven, and will forgive their sin and heal their land."* God hears us from heaven when we humbly pray, seek him, and turn from our sin.

Taking 2 Chronicles to heart myself, I went to confession that Saturday, thanking the Lord and asking him for the grace to keep me from sinning again.

NINETEEN

A Mighty Rushing Wind

Tom slowly approached the front of the small stuffy room. Facing the horseshoe shape of our small group, he methodically flipped through the thin pages of his bible to begin the Life in the Spirit Seminar. I could feel the excitement and anticipation pulse through the room as we sat waiting for him to begin.

After a short prayer inviting the Holy Spirit to be with us, and with the directness you would expect from a professional mathematician, Tom took a breath and began reading aloud from the second chapter of Acts.

Never will I forget that evening in early summer. Mary and I had joined a group of about thirty people in a small white meetinghouse on the campus of Immaculate Conception parish in Towson, Maryland. A few months earlier, Tom had called to ask if Mary and I would like to be team leaders for the upcoming seminar. We agreed instantly.

Of course, we were excited and thankful for this opportunity and were eager to serve the Lord together in a new ministry. I recall the two of us driving to Towson, filled with the same promise of a long-awaited first date.

And just like a first date, I remember every detail. I looked up at the beautiful starry sky of that still night before I entered the house. It had only two rooms and a small kitchen on the first floor, and, I quickly realized, there was no air conditioning,

As each person passed through the door of that little house, I could feel the temperature rising. A wave of anxiety came over me at the thought of getting overheated. The excessive sweating condition I had developed as a child was both uncomfortable and embarrassing. The Holy Spirit was certainly asking me for a sacrifice.

Thankfully, the team opened the windows and doors to attempt getting some air flowing through the rooms. But alas, the stillness of the night prevented so much as a breeze, perhaps just enough air to cool things down a bit.

As Tom began to read about Pentecost and how the Holy Spirit descended upon the Apostles for the first time, I pictured them clearly, all gathered together in a small room much like the one where we were sitting. *"And suddenly,"* Tom read, *"a sound came from heaven like the rush of a mighty wind, and it filled all the house where they were sitting."*

All at once, as if on cue, a mighty wind blasted through our room and broke the stillness of the evening. It rushed through the open windows and doors of the tiny house, shaking it with a fierce power. Windows rattled, and the doors slammed shut loudly. The simultaneous banging sounds all around us reverberated throughout the room.

We looked around at one another in wonder, wide eyes verifying that we all had just experienced the same incredible thing. Sitting stiffly in our chairs at the highest level of attention, we waited for someone to break the residual silence. I looked at Tom, who was just as dumbfounded as the rest of us. He stood there rubbing his arms, the way he does when he gets chills.

Someone had to say something! There was no question in my mind that the same Holy Spirit at Pentecost had just shown himself to us in a mighty way. Finally, I said the only thing that made sense, "This is going to be a powerful experience!"

It certainly was a powerful experience, in which I received many spiritual gifts in just two short days. I was filled with a desire to share what I had been given, and I was not alone in this sentiment. The spiritual experience was so moving that we had to share it with those around us. We needed others to see and believe, just as we had seen and believed.

The next day, we nearly doubled our number. Many came back to the seminar bringing others with them. I realized that this was precisely how the early Church in the Acts of the Apostles was formed. The Life in the Spirit Seminar showed me clearly the mission of our Christian faith, and I too joined in the apostolate we share.

Together we experienced the same incredible transformation, committing our lives to the service and obedience of Jesus Christ. For me personally, I can't tell you fully how significant the experience of that seminar really was in my own life. The forceful, rushing wind that shook the house during that incredible Life in the Spirit Seminar forty years ago also shook the very depths of my own spirit. For weeks after, the Holy Spirit worked in me, forever claiming me for Christ. Filled with a deeper reverence than ever before, my desire to testify to his name and his goodness was bursting forth from me.

TWENTY

Because,
I Was There

Years later, our *New Life* community was asked to lead a Life in the Spirit Seminar at St. Joan of Arc Church in Aberdeen, Maryland. I had been participating in these seminars for the past several years and loved watching Christ move through the participants, renewing their lives with a focus on God's love. Whenever anyone came with the smallest seed of doubt, the Holy Spirit took that doubt and transformed it. He certainly made his presence known at these seminars!

There were only about ten people who attended the St. Joan of Arc seminar, and as always, there were people extremely wary and doubtful. As we broke into small groups, one lady in my group named Alice, had no problem voicing her suspicions.

The idea of the Holy Spirit working in her life was off-putting and didn't seem to line up with her understanding of Catholicism. After all, she was a daily communicant, she regularly prayed the rosary, and she ultimately believed she didn't need anything else from God. So, why was Alice here?

I'm sure curiosity had a lot to do with many of the doubtful participants who showed up for the first presentation and signed their names to the roster. In many ways, the seminar always reminds me of the disciples going out among the Jews, presenting the gifts of the Holy Spirit to a curious but otherwise ritualistic people.

Bonnie and I were assigned to co-lead our small group, and despite Alice's constant challenges, we both were enjoying her resistant yet comical disposition thoroughly. Bonnie and I knew that often the ones who came with the strongest opposition had the greatest transformation, and we couldn't wait to see what the Holy Spirit had in store for Alice!

We delved right into the deep waters of the seminar, with this woman questioning everything along the way. I eventually got the nagging sense from God that he wanted to break through to Alice in particular and reveal himself to her in a powerful way.

As strong as her daily faith practices had been, it became clear they were in place to make her feel safe. Alice didn't want her faith challenged any further, so she remained very guarded.

Although curiosity had perhaps led her to the seminar in the first place, it became obvious that there was now something greater keeping her here. She returned faithfully for each of the six nights as we shared about God's unconditional love.

In emphasizing the need to accept Jesus as Lord of our lives, and to put this truth into practice, many of the participants began to be profoundly affected throughout the week.

Alice listened quietly and observed each night as the rest of our group discussed what was occurring in their lives. On the fifth night, Bonnie and I prayed over her, asking that she might receive a new outpouring of the Holy Spirit.

As we prayed, I had a vision of Alice sitting on the side of her bed, clutching a crucifix to her chest, just over her heart. I heard her say in prayer, "Lord, I give you my day." I shared this vision with her exactly as I had seen it, and she stared back at me with a look of utter shock.

"Why did you just say that?" she quickly asked, almost coming out of her seat.

"I don't know," I responded. "I just saw it in my mind."

Her brows furrowed, and she seemed to be looking beyond us, questioning what she had just heard. After a few moments of contemplation and several deep breaths, she softly told us that I had just recounted exactly what she says and does each morning when she wakes up.

"I sit on the edge of my bed, holding my crucifix tightly to my heart. Then I give my day to the Lord. But how could you possibly have known that?" her voice trailed off.

I waited a moment before asking, "What do you do next?"

She looked back up at me and replied, "I go about my day."

I challenged her further, "Do you ever wait and listen for God's direction on what he wants you to do with your day?"

This seemed absurd to her. Why would God communicate such a thing to me? "Are you crazy?" she snapped. "Do you think I have all day to sit on my bed and wait for God to talk to me?" My eyes widened in surprise as she angrily continued, "I have much too much to do!"

I knew Alice needed a gentler approach to opening herself further to the Lord's will, and this would be a process. "Okay. Then simply go through your day, from that moment on your bed," I instructed, "and look for God to show you what he has for you to do that day."

This seemed to be acceptable to her, and so she agreed to give it a try. I reassured her of God's great love for her, and especially of his real presence with her each day in the Eucharist. Yet, there was still something bothering me. The Holy Spirit was pushing for something more from this woman, and so I said, "The Holy Spirit keeps showing me that God wants to reveal himself to you through your obedience and faithfulness."

For the rest of the week, I couldn't help wondering what God was doing in Alice's life. Just maybe it would be her who would have something to share at our next meeting.

Sure enough, the following week, I noticed Alice standing just inside the entrance of the doorway, waving me over to her. As I approached, I invited her to join us as we were just about to start. She desperately wanted to talk to me, but I convinced her that we could talk after the meeting. She reluctantly joined us, saying, "Okay, but what I have to say to you is very important and private." To tell you the truth, I thought she was going to tell me she reported me to the pastor for something I said!

We started the session as a large group, which provided an opportunity for those who wanted to share short testimonies of how the Lord had been working in their lives. One of the beautiful things about the Life in the Spirit Seminar is that there often are many immediate spiritual changes, and the participants find it helpful to share these with each other.

One after another, men and women shared about the greater peace in their lives and renewed sense of God's presence. The very last person to speak was the lovely Alice. When I asked if she wanted to share, her eyes critically scanned each face in front of her before taking a deep breath.

"I wouldn't share this with anyone else except for the people in this room," she said poignantly. "Every Friday night around eleven, I call my sister and mother on a three-way conference call. It's something we have been doing for a while now," she began.

"This last Friday, I asked my sister to stay on the line after we finished our call. I wanted to tell her about Bonnie and Charles praying over me, and how Charles had known about what I did each morning without me ever having told him. 'I have to tell you about what happened to me tonight,' I whispered into the phone. My sister's voice seemed to be as soft and mysterious as mine.

'I know what happened to you tonight,' she said. 'Don't be silly,' I shot back. 'Just stay on the line after we talk to mom.'"

"Now it's important to know that we each live in different time zones," Alice emphasized. "We called and spoke to Mom, and after she hung up, my sister and I resumed our conversation." Our group was a captive audience, listening for what was about to be revealed.

"I repeated to my sister once again that I wanted to share with her what had happened to me that night, and she again said she knew what had happened. I couldn't understand why she kept insisting on this. Frustrated, I said, 'Well then, tell me what happened!'

"My sister's voice was clear and confident on the other end of the line. 'You were in a small room. Two other people were with you, and they were praying for you to receive an outpouring of the Holy Spirit,' she unexplainably recounted. Her words were like lightning as they struck me. Then she said, 'And you received it.'

"I was stunned. How could this be happening? How could she have known any of this? 'How do you know?' I questioned in a state of desperation, needing an answer. 'I can't explain it, Sister, but I was there,' she said."

We were all taken aback by Alice's incredible story, but even greater was the change I saw occurring in her. She was renewed in joy, completely transformed into a woman full of the joy brought only through a strong and growing personal relationship with Jesus. The Holy Spirit continued to work through her in many powerful ways. She discovered Jesus over and over again in prayer and shared many of these experiences with me.

One of the greatest lessons the Lord has taught me over the years, through prayer, is the need to wait and watch. I must be vigilant, always waiting for him to move, instruct, and lead. Even after prayer, there is a need to be still and wait, listening for his instruction. Sometimes God speaks clearly, directly answering "yes" or "no." Other times require greater patience, waiting through constant prayer to discover the revelation of his answer.

More important than the act of hearing his voice or experiencing a mystical encounter is his revelation to us through prayer. In prayer, we find the Lord's teaching and instruction, allowing us to understand his reasons. These are the greatest gifts along our spiritual journey toward full union with him. In this way, the life of Alice was radically changed. Christ became closer to her than her own heartbeat.

Pray, wait, watch, and listen.

> *"And he came and found them sleeping, and he said to Peter, "Simon, are you asleep? Could you not watch one hour? Watch and pray that you may not enter into temptation; the spirit indeed is willing, but the flesh is weak." (Mark 14:37-38)*

TWENTY-ONE

The Angel Visit

Our community was conducting what had now become our annual Life in the Spirit Seminar, this time at St. Ignatius in Hickory, Maryland. We were ready for whatever God threw our way as he transformed the lives of the participants. As always, we were expecting the unexpected.

Mike was an older man who had decided to go through the course, particularly prompted by something that was bothering him. Having been a facilitator at these seminars for more than eighteen years, I had witnessed many incredible transformations, and I had come to recognize that yearning for God that I saw in Mike.

When we separated into small groups, Mike and the men in my group listened as I shared. I could tell there was something very specific bothering Mike, and his anxiety regarding this matter seemed to grow as I spoke.

I informed the men that on the fifth week of the seminar we would pray for an outpouring of the Holy Spirit upon them. In faith, they should open themselves to the work of the Holy Spirit within them, ask God for an intention very important to them, and be prepared to receive his healing mercy and grace.

Mike grew more excited as each week passed. Throughout his long walk with God and the Catholic faith, there were many important things he had not yet learned and was now discovering. Again and again he would ask, "Why has no one ever told me this before?" But God had chosen this moment to open his eyes and make everything new again.

When the fifth week finally came, Mike was there with bells on! Two facilitators and I opened the meeting and began to pray for the Holy Spirit to come upon us. When it was Mike's turn for prayer, I leaned forward and asked him, "Mike, what is it you would like us to pray for?"

Mike tightened his mouth for a moment and then replied, "I want God to take away my terrible fear of dying." At last, I understood what was bothering this man, and why he was pursuing God so fervently near the end of his life. We prayed over him for this intention and ended with an "Amen."

The seminar wrapped up, and everyone happily returned to life as normal, yet renewed with fervent strength in the Lord! Mike and I kept in contact, remaining close to one another after our journey through the Life in the Spirit Seminar.

Three months passed, and one night Mary received a call from Sue, one of our community members. I was just sitting down to a lovely spaghetti dinner as Mary stared at me with the phone to her ear, prodding me to guess what she was hearing.

"What's going on?" I mouthed. Mary looked at me and said, "Mike is dying. Sue says his liver and kidney functions have shut down, and the doctors are only giving him hours to live."

I knew why Sue was calling. "She wants me to go and see him," I stated. "Yes," Mary confirmed, "right away!"

Pushing away from my beautiful dish of spaghetti, I drove the familiar road to the hospital. It was close to 10:00 PM by the time I arrived, and well past visiting hours. I was almost certain they wouldn't let me see Mike.

But as I walked toward Mike's wing, there were no nurses or doctors at the desk. I was able to walk freely, straight to his room. A group of women and one young man were standing in the hall just outside. They were crying hysterically, and they glanced back and forth at one another as I approached.

"Is this Mike's room?" I asked. They looked up at me startled, and for a moment they stopped weeping. "Who are you?" the young man asked skeptically. "I'm a friend of Mike's, and I would like to pray for him," I responded gently. One of the ladies was very unsure about me and said to the young man, "Go with him. I don't know who he is."

Walking through the door, I saw Mike laying in a recliner. I'll never forget the look in his eyes, filled with such a fear. Mike looked across the room at me and began to cry like a baby. I saw the fear wash away in an instant, as tears of joy filled his eyes. Not knowing what to say, I knelt and took his withered hands in mine. It was then that God revealed to me what he wanted Mike to hear. "Mike, God is freeing you from your fear of dying. You will physically recover from this ailment."

Mike smiled, and I left his hospital bed with strong faith and hope in his physical and spiritual recovery, knowing that God was working in his heart. Returning home to Mary and my spaghetti dinner, I rejoiced in the rest of the evening.

Mary received another call from Sue the next morning. "We have a miracle," Sue shouted into the phone. "An amazing miracle!" Mary's eyes lit up and a smile spread across her face. "When Mike awoke this morning, he was completely healed," Sue said, beside herself with excitement. "All of his functions have returned to normal!"

Hanging up the phone, Mary confirmed what I already knew; Mike was healed. I thanked the Lord, saying repeatedly, "What a mighty God you are!" Mike remained close to my heart, and about a year later he gave his testimony at St. Ignatius Church to the new participants and friends of the Life in the Spirit Seminar.

As he arose to speak, he looked at me directly. "This is my story," he began, "and part of my story has never been revealed to Charles." I was taken aback that there was more to his story, and reclining in the church pew, I waited excitedly to hear what had occurred between God and Mike.

"When Charles walked into the door of my room at the hospital," Mike began, "I didn't see him. What I saw was a bright light that filled the doorway. It came nearer and nearer, and then I saw Charles kneeling before me as he prayed with great power." Mike paused a moment to choke back the tears that were beginning to overtake him. "I knew he had come with an angel."

I think the shock on my face reflected how surprised I was that God had used me in such a way. God's ways are not our ways, and they are forever mysterious to us. In his great mystery, God sent an angel with me into Mike's hospital room to deliver that very special and personal message.

The real miracle of the story for Mike was not his physical healing, but the answering of his prayer. After the "angel visit," as he called it, Mike was completely healed from his fear of dying. It was not until several years later that Mike did, in fact, pass on peacefully and without fear, ready to welcome eternal life.

To this day I thank God that he sent an angel to be with me as I delivered his divine healing to Mike. I never truly understand what God is doing in the moment, yet just like all of us, I earnestly desire the higher gifts of God and resist fear when God does choose to use them in me. As Christians, we must show up with him and witness his power. That's what I did with Mike.

Thus far, I have experienced two similar miracles concerning the intervention of angels. This has led me to heed the warning in Hebrews 13:2: *"Do not neglect to show hospitality to strangers, for thereby some have entertained angels unawares."*

TWENTY-TWO

The Red Roses

I am always very comforted in knowing that God has my Mary in the palm of his hand. The Lord certainly has a tender spot in his heart for this woman, for he has shed his healing grace upon her many times. That's why I didn't worry about her annual mammogram, even when a call from Dr. King was transferred to my office phone two days later.

I knew that Dr. King was Mary's doctor, and I guessed he probably lost our home phone number and was trying to reach her. But this was not the case.

The doctor needed to tell me directly that Mary had breast cancer. Despite his gentle way of delivering the news, I collapsed in my chair and began to weep profusely. So much so, that a young man who worked with me rushed into my office to see what was wrong. When I told him, he placed his arms around me, giving me the only comfort he knew at the moment.

I truly was a wreck. Doubt and fear began assaulting my thoughts, drastically challenging my faith. "How can I tell my beloved?" I thought as I went home to her. As much as I tried to prevent it, my eyes began to well with tears at her joyful greeting.

Mary could tell something was wrong, and sitting with her on the couch, I delicately told her what Dr. King had said. We both began to cry, and I held her in the midst of our soft weeping. After a short time, Mary stood up, somehow strengthened, and boldly declared, "So be it." That's my Mary! She constantly reminds me of the commitment we made to have absolute trust and faith in our Lord, in good times and in bad. Recalling how

he had healed her of a breast tumor many years before, I began
to pray ardently and listened for God's word. But no revelation
came. I could only wait patiently in faith.

I didn't know what God was doing, but I reasoned that, in spite
of myself, it was something very powerful. Mary was renewed in
peace after our community prayed over her, but I was still very
impatient, waiting for God to tell me something–anything.
His silence was deafening.

Mary decided to pray a novena to St. Thérèse, for whom she had
a special affection. She secretly hoped the saint, known as the
Little Flower would send her a gift of roses to assure her of
God's healing presence. She pleaded with the heavenly courts
for a full recovery.

After receiving the sacrament of Extreme Unction from our
parish priest, Mary grew in the strength she needed to face her
ordeal. Devoted to prayer and filled with hope in Christ, Mary
and I went to the hospital to have her breast removed. The cancer
was spreading quickly, and yet we were full of trust in what God
was about to do in her fragile life. We knew that the Holy Spirit
was there with her and the physicians.

Knowing her devotion to St. Thérèse and the novena she was
completing, I decided to find a florist and get a vase of roses
to place before her when she woke up from her anesthesia.
Walking the streets of Baltimore on this mission gave me a
reason not to fixate on the surgery.

The nice ladies at the small hidden flower shop I found tucked
away on a side street gave me a beautiful crystal vase with a
big red ribbon and bow. With the twelve red roses surrounded by
baby's breath, the arrangement was quite lovely and distinctive.
As a finishing touch, I asked them to inscribe a message on the
little card that would accompany the roses, "From an angel
who loves you."

I entered her room and placed the roses on the bed tray. I wanted them to be the first thing Mary saw when she opened her eyes, as an answer to her novena that she would fully recover.

I waited happily next to her bedside, and as she slowly awoke, I watched her eyes flutter and open upon the vision of the roses. She looked at the vase and softly said, "Roses! Who sent them?"

Nodding toward the card, I said proudly, "It says an angel." Then after a short pause, I continued, "And that angel...is me!" I confessed.

Her eyes reflected a moment's disappointment before she gently said, "But Honey, you knew I had prayed a novena to St. Thérèse."

Quickly trying to reassure her, I said in my defense, "Well, there are many ways God can answer a novena, even through me."

I knew it wasn't what she truly wanted to hear, but she graciously said, "Thank you, Honey," all the same.

I sat in the chair next to her bed, holding her small hand in mine. It was a sweet moment that was interrupted when a nurse briskly entered the room. She was carrying a crystal vase much like the one I had just given to Mary. The vase also was decorated with a big red ribbon and bow, and it also contained twelve red roses surrounded by baby's breath!

Upon further examination, I realized this was exactly the same arrangement I had purchased from the obscure little flower shop. It was the same even down to the crystal vase.

Mary's eyes came alive again when she beheld the second bouquet of roses. "Roses!" she cried out again. "Who sent them?"

I was just as interested in this answer as she was. My first inclination was that the florist had made some kind of mistake, accidentally sending over a duplicate of my order. I quickly reached for the small card peeking out from the sea of baby's breath. It read, "From Aunt Mary and Uncle Paul."

"Aunt Mary and Uncle Paul?" I thought. "How in the world did Aunt Mary and Uncle Paul find the same florist...and then choose the same custom arrangement, vase, and bow?" My mind was blown.

I walked over to the window and looked down at the street below. "What is this Lord?" I asked. "What are you telling me?"

His reply was swift and simple, *"I didn't ask for your help."*

I realized then that my trust in him had been weak. I knew Mary was praying the novena, but I somehow felt I had to make this miracle happen for her. In the end, it amounted to nothing more than another self-fulfilling prophecy, very shallow at best.

Yet God rose above it all! He came through for Mary despite my interference, teaching me a great lesson in unfailing trust. God showed me that sometimes he is too small in my mind, and through a crystal vase of red roses, he showed me that he doesn't need me to do the miracles for him.

> *"He whose Heart ever watcheth, taught me, that while for a soul whose faith equals but a tiny grain of mustard seed, He works miracles, in order that this faith which is so weak may be fortified." (St. Thérèse)*

TWENTY-THREE

The Wedding Song

The Lord's gift of music to my family and me is something I have deeply loved and cherished. No longer on a big stage in front of many adoring fans, I now play my guitar and sing for the Lord, giving praise and thanksgiving to him alone.

Early one morning, as my music rose up in prayer to him, the words and melody of a song began to form in my mind. Grabbing a scrap of paper, I wrote feverishly as the lyrics seemed to flow from my thoughts like water being poured out of a jug.

I wanted to capture them all, ensuring I wouldn't lose or forget what I was hearing. God was telling me something important, and the words seemed very significant.

> *For God loves us so, that he gave us his Son*
> *So that we might be one, and live in him.*
> *To trust in his word, the truth we have heard*
> *That Jesus Christ is Lord.*
> *And now we are one, for the Father and Son*
> *And the Spirit has come to unite us.*
> *Through Jesus the Way, we'll love and obey*
> *And stay in the presence of God.*
> *For God loves you so, that he gave you his Son*
> *So that you may be one, and be in him*
> *And walk in his light, on your path through the night*
> *To the glorious sight of his face.*

After finishing the song, I deeply reflected on the words. It was then that I was struck by a profound clarity of revelation–

the words were for a wedding song. They were meant for someone who was soon to be married.

I racked my brain, trying to remember if anyone I knew was getting married, but no one came to mind. "Why have you inspired me to write a wedding song, Lord?" I asked.

At last I recalled that Dave and Suzanne, a couple in our community, were about to enter into the Sacrament of Matrimony. I decided to step out in faith and ask them if this song was meant for them. After all, they were the only people I knew who were getting married, and I thought that maybe God wanted to give them this song.

After our next prayer meeting, I asked the couple if I could speak with them. Pulling them aside, I told them that I had gotten a song from the Lord. "I'm not sure, but I think this song may have been written for you," I told them. "It just came to me one morning while I was singing to the Lord," I said. "I wonder if you guys would listen to it and ask God if he gave this song to you for your wedding."

They were both anxious to hear it, and grabbing my guitar, I started to sing. As I sang the words to them, Suzanne began to cry. It was clear to both Dave and I that the song was increasingly affecting her as I sang on.

When I finished, I asked her if she was okay. Smiling and crying at the same time, she said, "I prayed that God would give us a song for our wedding, and I prayed that it would come through you."

God used me to answer Suzanne's prayer, and he allowed my music to be a gift of his love to another. Thank you, Lord!

"When I look at thy heavens, the work of thy fingers, the moon and the stars which thou hast established; what is man that thou art mindful of him, and the son of man that thou dost care for him?"

"Yet thou hast made him little less than God, and dost crown him with glory and honor. Thou hast given him dominion over the works of thy hands; thou hast put all things under his feet." (Psalm 8:3-6)

TWENTY-FOUR

Under the Spout

One fall semester, my son Aaron invited Mary and me to Franciscan University, where he was studying. He was interested in Theresa, a girl he really wanted us to meet. She was from a well-to-do family of devout Catholics, and despite attending a leading Charismatic college, she really didn't understand the Charismatic Renewal or its place in the Church. With that knowledge, and given our expressive charismatic spirituality, I thought, "This certainly will prove interesting."

Aaron introduced his friend when we arrived, and the four of us made our way to the chapel for Mass. As Father Michael Scanlan climbed the stairs of the altar, I realized how thankful I was for having heard him speak so many years prior, at the Catholic Charismatic Conference in Atlantic City. Micah and Joshua had already graduated from the University, so I was used to seeing Father Michael regularly. But I still felt as deeply moved by his words as I had that first time.

When it came to the final announcements after Mass, Father Michael invited everyone to join him in the Student Center. There he would be giving an explanation and demonstration on the charismatic gifts of the Holy Spirit.

I was so excited! Who better to learn from than Father Michael himself? This was the perfect opportunity for Theresa to learn more about the Charismatic Renewal. Father Michael was not only the president of the University, but he also was a deeply holy priest, rooted in the love of God and the gifts of the Holy Spirit.

I excitedly turned to Theresa and said, "Come with me. God has two seats waiting for us, right under the spout where the glory comes out!"

She laughed nervously and asked, "What are you getting me into, Mr. Piccirilli?"

With that, Mary, Aaron, Theresa, and I made our way across the grass to the Student Center with almost the entire congregation. We did our best to squeeze into the back of the large room, which already was packed. Crammed in like sardines, people were standing against the doors and overflowing into the hallway.

My first reaction was frustration, because I really wanted to get Theresa near the front of that room. Instead, we were stuck in the very back of the room where it was hard to see and hear.

Suddenly, Father Michael yelled out, "There are two seats right here up front, under the spout where the glory comes out."

Well, I knew that was from the Lord, and so I immediately yelled back to him, "Father, those seats are for us!" I grabbed Theresa's hand and dragged her behind me, all the way to the front row.

Father Michael began speaking about the gifts of the Spirit in his animated nature, especially teaching on the gift of tongues. Then he encouraged everyone in the room to make noise, as if their favorite football team had just scored a touchdown.

"Cheer for that team!" he shouted loudly as the room erupted in cheer. When we all became quiet once again, he instructed, "Now do that without using words."

We sat dumbfounded for a few moments before again erupting in a collective expression of spirited emotion, only this time without words. We were motioning, raising our hands, and making noises of delight.

The room again quieted, although we kept smiling at those near us, all of us feeling equally as foolish. Father Michael then said, "That is an example of what the gift of tongues might sound like to us. We each need to be open to loving God with our whole heart as well as our mouth. Let the Holy Spirit praise God through you."

That night, Theresa said she encountered the Holy Spirit in an unexplainable way, and she too received the gift of tongues.

Have you ever wondered what the voices of heaven sound like? Would there be many different languages, or only one? I had a dream when I was a young man in which I was being lifted from earth toward heaven. As I rose into the deep blue starlit sky, I heard a faint hum that sounded like the sustained note of a single violin string, or the hum of a human voice.

As my body ascended closer to what I knew was God's throne, I began to hear a subtle staccato within the sound, gradually breaking apart into the sound of a muttering crowd.

Finally, just before waking from the dream, I heard the overpowering joy of millions of voices singing praise to God in as many voices as there were people. Listening, I never recognized a single language among all those many voices. Yet, I knew unquestioningly they were all glorifying God. Then I awoke.

A glimpse of heaven? Maybe so, but after twenty plus years of having the gift of tongues, I find I am just beginning to understand how the gift of tongues at Pentecost has something to do with Babel.

Starting with Genesis and in God's original plan for humanity, the whole earth spoke with one tongue. Yet, as the people's pride grew and they began to build a tower to reach God by their own human power, God confounded their language. No longer could they understand one another, and this confusion of speech led to their scattering abroad. (Genesis 11:1-9)

Pentecost is the antithesis of Babel. At Pentecost, each person understood what the other was saying, because the Holy Spirit interpreted the divine language of love. At Babel, the people worked to reach the kingdom of heaven through their own strength and pride. At Pentecost they allowed God to work through them in their weakness and humility. Thus, all present were united with Christ.

When Jesus commissioned the disciples, he said,

> *"And these signs will accompany those who believe: in my name they will cast out demons; they will speak in new tongues; they will pick up serpents, and if they drink any deadly thing, it will not hurt them; they will lay their hands on the sick, and they will recover."*
> *(Mark 16:17-18)*

That same Spirit moves through many of us who believe when, in humility, we allow him. He comes with the gentleness of a dove and the force of a hurricane. Could the gift of tongues be a taste of the heavenly language God gave men before Babel?

> *"God has appointed in the church first apostles, second prophets, third teachers, then workers of miracles, then healers, helpers, administrators, speakers in various kinds of tongues." (1 Corinthians 12:27-31)*

It is imperative in all of this, however, that we understand that love is always the aim. We might not always understand God, but when we earnestly desire these spiritual gifts entrusted to us by the Holy Spirit, we show God our trust and love.

These special graces, called charisms, are extraordinary gifts, *"oriented toward sanctifying grace and are intended for the common good of the Church. They are at the service of charity which builds up the Church." (CCC 2003).*

Yet, I can't pray in the Spirit if my mind is blank or unfruitful, like a musical instrument playing random notes, unarranged in any musical score. The resulting noise is appropriately unappreciated and confusing. To this no one can say "Amen."

> *"If I speak in the tongues of men and of angels, but*
> *have not love, I am a noisy gong or a clanging*
> *cymbal. And if I have prophetic powers, and understand all*
> *mysteries and all knowledge, and if I have all faith, so as*
> *to remove mountains, but have not love, I am nothing. If I*
> *give away all I have, and if I deliver my body to be burned,*
> *but have not love, I gain nothing."*
> *(1 Corinthians 13:1-3)*

The true gift at Pentecost had hardly to do with languages at all, but everything to do with the healing freedom of the confusion and disobedience manifested at the tower of Babel.

TWENTY-FIVE

Happy Mother's Day

Mary began complaining about a new pain she was feeling in her side. We both hoped it was something that would go away by the next morning, but it continued throughout the next few days. By the end of the week, it became difficult for her to even walk or stand, and she made an immediate appointment with our family physician.

After explaining the quick progression of pain to the doctor, Mary was sent for an x-ray and MRI. The images revealed that she had a very serious mass in her side. The doctor set up an appointment for her to see a surgeon right away, and off we went.

Bad news seemed to follow us. The surgeon who studied the images of Mary's side and thoroughly examined her said, "You have a hard tumor about the size of a small football in your side. I hope you realize this must be removed immediately, especially considering its size and rate of growth." As I allowed the doctor's words to penetrate my mind and my heart, I realized that I despised the seriousness in his voice, and I hated the words, "immediate surgery," but here we were...again.

Mary thankfully was still Mary, and she confidently had her own agenda. She was not afraid to pipe right up and say, "I'm not going in for any surgery until I first go to prayer group and get prayer for healing." And that is exactly what she did. I give her so much credit for this, because the Holy Spirit always comes first for Mary, even when her feet are in the fire.

That Sunday, Mary not only received prayer for healing, but she also received the sacrament of the Anointing of the Sick. When we awoke Monday morning, Mary said to me, "Honey, I am feeling somewhat better."

This filled us both with hope, as I exclaimed, "Maybe God is healing you!"

We remained hopeful for the remainder of the day, and when she woke up on Tuesday, Mary joyfully remarked, "I am really feeling better! The pain has subsided a lot."

We knew in prudence that we needed to call our family physician and find out what was medically occurring with Mary's tumor, but we also trusted in our hearts that God was working.

When she called the doctor and reported the diminishing symptoms, he wasn't quite sure why Mary wasn't experiencing a worsening pain from the tumor, and perhaps he assumed it was just wishful thinking. He scheduled her for another MRI on Thursday. Returning home from getting those scans, we knew we had all our bases covered. We just had to wait on the Lord.

Mary was looking forward to the following Sunday, which was Mother's Day. She fully planned to enjoy the day with her three boys and celebrate her motherhood. Together, we waited in hope for the results of the MRI. Friday seemed to wash in and out like a wave on the sand, the kind that you just watch in peace and silence. And then finally on Friday evening, word came by way of our family doctor. The results were in.

Mary asked him to please wait for a moment while she got a chair. I knew she was nervous despite her calm demeanor, and she needed to sit down in case the news was bad. But there was no need for a chair, at least not for bad news.

The doctor's voice could not be silenced another moment, as he exclaimed, "Mary, your tumor is gone! In fact, it's not only gone, but there is no sign it was ever there." Mary and I were overcome by immense joy and just looked at each other, the way we have come to do when we experience a miracle. We were speechless, but then the doctor's voice found the perfect words to say. "Happy Mother's Day, Mary."

We rejoiced and rejoiced in the Mother's Day gift of healing from the Lord. We had learned by now that God's gifts are abundant and plentiful, but still as new and beautiful as the dawn. One man, however, did not yet know this–Mary's surgeon.

I remember him calling the week after we received the happy news. He was both startled and confused, as he said, "It is impossible for the tumor to have disappeared. I know it is there. I felt it with my own two hands." He certainly wasn't going to let this slide on a supernatural ticket, especially suspecting medical negligence. "I want you in my office right away so that I can personally review those films," his voice boomed through the phone.

So, Mary and her sister Rose went together to his office the following day. Mary sat once again on the exam table in her gown as the surgeon pushed and prodded her body for several minutes. He was determined to find the mass he had found so easily at our earlier visit. As he looked from the films to Mary's side, he seemed to become more anxious. At last, he said to her, "Well, I know it's there, even if I can't find it now."

Mary and her sister left the office with even greater confirmation of the Mother's Day miracle! They could certainly understand why the surgeon was extremely dumbfounded by a tumor of that size disappearing so quickly and without a trace, but God is like that. And so, we praise his name–

> *"Bless the Lord, O my soul; And all that is within me*
> *bless his holy name! Bless the Lord, O my soul,*
> *And forget not all his benefits, Who forgives all your*
> *iniquity, Who heals all your diseases, Who redeems*
> *your life from the Pit, Who crowns you with steadfast*
> *love and mercy, Who satisfies you with good as long as*
> *you live, So that your youth is renewed like the eagle's."*
> *(Psalm 103)*

TWENTY-SIX

The Healing of Ashley

The day Rose and Bob's granddaughter Ashley was born, her mother Michelle just knew in her spirit that something wasn't quite right with her beautiful little daughter. Despite a smooth birth and constant reassurance from the medical team that Ashley was perfectly healthy, Michelle had a hidden unrest within that she couldn't reconcile.

Michelle and Scott brought Ashley home to meet her older brother Jake, who was overjoyed to have a baby sister. Yet as hard as they tried to ignore Ashley's frightening health symptoms over the next four months, Michelle and Scott couldn't deny that she was very different from how Jake had been in his first year of life. Ashley would projectile vomiting sporadically, and sometimes she would do so upon waking.

Michelle constantly brought these concerns to Ashley's pediatrician, who always assured her that nothing was wrong. In fact, as Michelle's worry for her daughter's condition increased and she pushed the doctors to pay attention to the unusual symptoms, the pediatrician began to wonder if Michelle was a hypochondriac.

By Ashley's nine-month check-up, she still had not begun crawling or hitting any of the milestones of most babies her age. A finger prick blood test revealed that Ashley had low iron, so the pediatrician prescribed supplements for anemia and told her parents that there was nothing else wrong. However, shortly after the check-up, Ashley's vomiting worsened, warranting yet another call to the doctor. This time, he advised Scott and Michelle to take their daughter to a hematologist at the University of Maryland just to be sure.

The hematologist ran an x-ray on Ashley and assured Michelle and Scott that the enlarged liver they saw in the film was no cause for alarm. It seemed to be nothing more than a blood disorder. Michelle's motherly instinct continued to tell her that something was terribly wrong with her daughter, but she could not find a medical ally to take her concerns seriously.

The hematologist they were seeing at the University of Maryland left his position shortly after Ashley's x-ray, and another specialist took his place. Finally, God made himself abundantly clear to Michelle through this new hematologist, who happened to be from the same town in Minnesota where she had grown up. The two bonded immediately, and Michelle finally felt at peace, now that her daughter was in his care.

When Ashley's new doctor told Michelle he wanted to see her in his office right away, she and Rose left for the University of Maryland with Ashley for an official examination with the new hematologist. The doctor knew something wasn't right the moment he lifted Ashley's shirt to examine her abdomen. Ashley's stomach was severely distended, and even to the naked eye, the doctor recognized the veins protruding through the skin around her liver. "What we're dealing with is cancer," he said plainly.

Rose and Michelle gasped. What more could be said on that Wednesday in February? The reason for the hidden unrest in Michelle's spirit, which had been growing since her daughter's birth, had been confirmed. Rose and Michelle were told that the iron supplements had enhanced the growth of her type of cancer dramatically, causing the tumor to increase rapidly. This had worked in their favor, however, because it made her condition abundantly clear to the hematologist, rather than disguising it as a blood disorder. "We will pray," Rose assured her. "The whole community will be praying."

That Friday, February 13, 1998, Mary and I received the alarming call from Rose. "Ashley has cancer," she spoke through tears on the other line. "Michelle and Scott have been with her at the hospital these past three days. The doctors ran a battery of tests on her," Rose continued. Mary held her hand over her mouth to stop herself from making a sound, as her face began to drop.

"The surgeon showed them the x-rays, CT scan, and MRI this afternoon," Rose's voice was faint now. "Ashley has Hepatoblastoma, and Monday morning she will have surgery to remove a massive tumor in her liver."

Mary caught her breath and asked, "What does this mean, Rose?" There was a slight pause.

"If the surgery is successful and chemotherapy can eradicate the cancer, her liver can regenerate," Rose answered with the first hopeful glimmer in all the bleak news.

Rose asked Mary and me to join her and Bob and the rest of the community at Michelle and Scott's house after the noon Mass on Sunday to pray over Ashley. We emphatically agreed. On Sunday, we pulled out of the St. Ignatius parking lot; followed family, friends, and New Life community members; and made our way to the home of little Ashley.

Michelle and Scott welcomed us into their living room, where ten-month-old Ashley was nestled in her mother's lap, watching each of us as we entered. Community members gathered around the room as their voices erupted in tongues of prayer. I noticed that Michelle began to cry softly as Ashley contently moved back and forth between her parents for the half hour we prayed with them. Watching this family, I knew in my spirit just how strongly Christ desired this type of communal prayer in the Church. The gathering together of so many faithful Christians in the small living room allowed me to see clearly how the Lord was enveloping this family in his loving embrace.

As we lifted Ashley's little body to the Lord in prayer, asking for her healing, I was listening deeply for the Lord to speak. I was so thankful when his voice finally came to me, saying, *"This disease will not end her life. She will grow to be a healthy woman of God."*

My happiness at his words made it almost impossible to speak. "The Lord has said to me that this cancer will not end Ashley's life!" I proclaimed joyfully. I heard many whispers around me thanking Jesus, and then softly and through tears, I heard Michelle's personal thanksgiving spoken to the Lord for her daughter's life.

That evening Michelle and Scott took Ashley to be admitted at the University of Maryland Medical Center. When the surgeon met with them early the next morning, just before surgery, he gave them a hopeful prognosis. Somehow the tumor was completely encapsulated and not attached to any of the neighboring organs. It was lying on top of Ashley's organs and not growing into them. This was certainly a miraculous finding, which significantly increased Ashley's chances of a full recovery.

That morning was agonizing for all of us as we waited for the news to come. For eight and a half hours, Michelle and Scott paced the waiting room, visited the chapel, and did whatever they could to endure the seemingly endless time their little girl was in surgery.

Finally, the surgeon passed through the doors into the waiting area with a look of relief on his face. "We were able to remove the tumor entirely," he began. "It weighed more than two pounds, which explains why Ashley never crawled or met other milestones. It also was necessary to remove ninety percent of Ashley's liver, but I expect that it will regenerate in several years.

The major part of the surgery was spent repairing the wall of Ashley's liver."

The couple embraced one another, and Michelle asked immediately, "Can we see her?"

As Michelle and Scott entered the pediatric ICU where Ashley lay unconscious in her recovery bed, Michelle gasped at how awful her little baby looked. The color was drained from her skin and once rosy cheeks. For the next two days, Michelle and Scott took turns sitting beside her bed, watching over their child, as she remained sedated to control the pain.

At last, Ashley's breathing tube was removed, and she was able to transfer to a step-down unit from the ICU. They could now hold and cradle their baby in their arms, while navigating a mass of wires. Many family and friends visited, but it was Michelle's father who had the most difficult time seeing Ashley in this condition. Upon entering the recovery room, he immediately looked away, unable to see her connected to so many wires. He sat for hours at the end of her bed, staring at her tiny foot, caressing and kissing it tenderly.

Ashley slowly regained consciousness and began to interact with her family, but not one of them could get her to crack a smile. She remained solemn for the rest of the week, up until the day before her discharge. Her father fondly remembers watching her smile for the first time since her surgery, when they put a Barney video on the television in her room.

One by one, on her last day in the hospital, the wires were removed, and Ashley was cleared for release. Her parents brought her home at last, and they snuggled close together with her older brother Jake, holding one another on the same living room floor where we had prayed so fervently only a week before.

The family celebrated Ashley's life and her successful surgery, recognizing the Lord's blessing upon them. All too soon,

Michelle and Scott reluctantly brought Ashley back to the hospital to begin the first of her six rounds of chemotherapy. It was a brutal time for all of them, especially brave little Ashley, who suffered nine of the ten rare side effects, attached to the treatment and had to be hospitalized for infection after each round of chemotherapy.

After only her second or third round of chemo, her blood work revealed that one of her liver numbers was skyrocketing. An MRI, however, clarified the unbelievable news that her liver already had mostly regenerated, something the doctors' thought would take much longer.

The *New Life* community continued to surround Ashley and her family with both prayer and presence during the months of her chemo and hospitalizations. Community members prepared meals and brought them to Michelle and Scott for months to come, and they took turns sitting for hours with Ashley and her parents in the hospital.

The healing of Ashley and the gratitude of Michelle and Scott on behalf of their family through this ordeal provided a vital lesson for all of us in the community. We discovered once again how absolutely we are one body in Christ.

"Having gifts that differ according to the grace given to us, let us use them: if prophecy, in proportion to our faith; if service, in our serving; he who teaches, in his teaching; he who exhorts, in his exhortation; he who contributes, in liberality; he who gives aid, with zeal; he who does acts of mercy, with cheerfulness."
(Romans 12:6-8)

The Lord's words were true to me that day in Ashley's living room, when she was only ten months old. The disease did not end her life, and she has grown into a healthy woman of God, just as he promised. Ashley just celebrated her nineteenth birthday, and she hasn't been back to the hospital for follow-up since she was six years old!

Ashley feels called by God to serve others through her own life as a pediatric oncology nurse. She is in her second year of a nursing program and recently had the incredible opportunity to return to the same oncology unit at the University of Maryland where she spent many weeks of her own childhood. She shadowed the daughter of a community member who is a nurse there and walked the hospital floors decorated with bright and happy pictures meant to comfort the scared families. Ashley couldn't help but look for a special nurse practitioner named Diane, who was the nurse who had cared for her nineteen years earlier. Ashley had heard so much about Diane from her mother, and she just knew she had to see her. When at last she spotted Diane, the shocked nurse recognized Ashley at once. Diane stopped everything and embraced Ashley as they both cried and held each other close.

> "The Lord is my strength and my shield;
> in him my heart trusts;
> so I am helped, and my heart exults,
> and with my song I give thanks to him."
> (Psalm 28:7)

TWENTY-SEVEN

Brush the Mole Away

One of our prayer group leaders stood up at a Sunday meeting and humbly told us of a concerning mole under his wife's eye. It had become hard and was beginning to turn red. As long as I had known Katherine, she had had that mole on her face.

At his request, we burst forth in prayer for Katherine, raising our voices up to the Lord. As we prayed, her husband stood up once again and said, "The Lord just told me to brush the mole away."

This seemed a bit strange, but we were used to strange by now at our prayer meetings. We never doubt the Lord's ability to speak or work through any one of us, so for the next thirty minutes, we prayed as he faithfully knelt before his wife and gently brushed her mole with his fingers.

At the close of the meeting, however, the mole was still there. Seeing no change on Katherine's face, someone stood up and said, "Maybe we all are supposed to brush it away!" Katherine endured this ritual with the patience of a saint. She stood stoically at the threshold of a doorway and allowed each community member to brush her cheek before leaving the meeting. She was hoping for a miracle.

Our community had two meetings that week—our Sunday gathering and an outreach meeting on Friday night. As we began to fill the room that Friday, I watched Katherine enter with her hand covering her cheek. She walked right over to me and said, "Look, Charles!"

When she moved her hand away, I could see that her skin was perfectly clear. "It's gone!" I said in amazement. There was no blemish, no red spot, and no sign at all of her life-long mole.

At our regular prayer meeting, Katherine stood up to give her testimony and to claim the miracle she had experienced. "I feel that in addition to my own healing, God wants to heal all suspicious moles today," she added. We sat for a moment with eyebrows raised awkwardly as she asked excitedly, "Okay, who has a mole?"

Nervous laughter filled the room as we looked around at each other uncomfortably. Then one woman named Priscilla said, "I have a mole on my arm." I was looking over at Mary, who for many years had a red mole on her cheek. "Mary has one," I said, as her head spun around in my direction. We all joined Katherine and began to pray for Priscilla and Mary.

The next morning, Mary was in the bathroom and called me. "Honey, come here and look. Something is happening to my mole!" Sure enough, the mole on her face was mysteriously changing color. Remembering that Katherine's mole required a little rubbing, Mary grabbed a washcloth and brushed it gently over the mole and rinsed her face. Within days it healed completely, just as Katherine's had done. Soon after, there was no mark or scar, just smooth skin.

Mary was not the only one joining Katherine in giving testimony to her miraculous healing at our next prayer meeting. Priscilla also showed us that the Lord had removed the mole from her arm as well.

God surely works in mysterious ways when we say "yes" to his promptings, even to the smallest details of our flesh.

"Truly, truly, I say to you, he who believes in me will also do the works that I do; and greater works than these will he do, because I go to the Father. Whatever you ask in my name, I will do it, that the Father may be glorified in the Son; if you ask anything in my name, I will do it." (John 14:12-14)

TWENTY-EIGHT

Thorns & Roses

I hope you are already aware that the saints are with us all the time. Without their constant intercession, particularly that of little St. Thérèse, Mary and I certainly wouldn't be this far along on our spiritual journey.

That's why it had such an impact on me when our very good friend Father Alphonse Rose, the priest who baptized Aaron, experienced a Thérèse miracle of his own.

The beautiful story of God working through Father Rose and St. Thérèse in the life of one woman was so confounding that it subsequently was documented in the *Catholic Review*. Shortly before his recent passing, I called Father Rose to ask his permission to share the story with you.

As chaplain at The Johns Hopkins Hospital, Father Rose was quite familiar with the sadness and tears of suffering loved ones. On one particular occasion, he encountered Claire, a seventy-four-year-old woman who was crying in a huddled heap in a chapel chair.

The old woman lifted her head when she heard him walk into the chapel, and she watched him through her tears as he took a seat. She followed her intuition and walked over and sat beside him. Although a faithful Methodist, Claire found great comfort in sitting in the presence of the priest and telling him about her son Dennis. Dennis had renal cell cancer and was facing an upcoming skull tumor operation.

Father Rose listened compassionately to the mother of the ill young man and prayed with her, asking the Lord to guide the surgeon's hands. He also prayed for comfort and strength for Claire throughout the difficult waiting period.

Claire had a prayer card of St. Thérèse of Lisieux that a friend had given her. She hoped to receive encouragement from St. Thérèse, and she believed that the Little Flower would send her "a rose from the heavenly garden…as a message of love."

As Father slowly stood to leave the chapel, Claire smiled at him and asked, "What is your name, Father?" "It's Father Rose," he replied.

Claire was astounded and felt the need to explain why she was in awe. She told him that she had asked for the intercession of St. Thérèse after receiving the holy card from a Catholic friend. She needed some sort of a sign or connection to heaven so she would be assured that God had indeed heard her prayers for Dennis. She had prayed for a rose.

"My dear, you have been praying for Thérèse to send you a rose, and I am 'A. Rose,'" said Father Alphonse Rose.

As they spoke, another woman who had entered the chapel overheard some of their conversation. As Father Rose left the chapel, the woman leaned over to Claire and quietly handed her a copy of the paper she had been reading just moments ago.

Claire was surprised to read the headline of an article about St. Thérèse, and as chills formed goose bumps on both of her arms, she looked back up at the woman, totally speechless. "I know," said the woman, affirming the strange coincidence. "If that isn't enough," she said, "my name is Thérèse."

With all that had happened in that little chapel, Claire was not surprised to learn that Dennis survived the surgery. He lived for another two years. Heaven had answered her, and she felt secure in the will of God for herself and Dennis. Claire's deep faith had been tested before, particularly when her husband left her and their young children, and when another son was killed in a car accident at the age of seventeen.

The Little Flower became a close, personal, heavenly friend to Claire, who again turned to her on her own behalf. Years after Dennis passed away, Claire suffered a series of strokes that severely impaired her vision. She also had emphysema, and the strokes complicated her dependence on an oxygen tank. This time, Claire asked St. Thérèse to send down a shower of roses from heaven, and if it be the will of God, to restore her vision.

She prayed fervently over the next few months from the confines of her lounge chair. One day, she felt well enough to venture out onto her back porch. As she made her way through the doorway, a lovely fragrance drew her attention to a branch from her neighbor's mulberry tree, which was hanging just above her. The branch was filled with a cluster of bright pink roses!

Claire thought immediately of Thérèse and smiled from ear to ear. Once inside, she could still see the roses through the window from her lounge chair, although that seemed impossible, with her diminished vision. She began to share this strange happening with others, and her house quickly became a pilgrimage for friends, family, and neighbors alike.

Perhaps her neighbors with the mulberry tree were the most baffled, as their tree had never before produced flowers. This bunch hanging over Claire's porch was the only one.

Among the pilgrims were Father John Lavin C.Ss.R., as well as Claire's pastor, Rev. Jeff Paulson. The two men photographed the roses and searched in vain to find the source of the rose's vine. When friends insisted that Claire pick a rose to keep for herself, she refused, because she thought them too holy to disturb.

And just as quickly as they had appeared, two weeks later, the roses were gone–without so much as a trace of a dead blossom on the ground or the original vine.

Claire wrote an account of her heavenly experiences with St. Thérèse and sent copies to at least two hundred people she knew. Her desire was not for them to get caught up in the miraculous, but rather that they be drawn toward God, knowing that he really does hear and answer our prayers. The God we serve gives life and takes it away, but through it all, he has a plan for each of us.

In 2003, Claire told the *Catholic Exchange* her story, explaining that, "I've always had faith, I had faith in order to survive. But it's gotten deeper and deeper. I've lost my vision, but I can see more clearly now than I ever could, if you know what I mean. I'm so happy, so thrilled, I'm so rich. There's nothing, absolutely nothing in this world that I need. I have it all, and I am at complete peace with God. I have no fears, I have no anxieties, and I have St. Thérèse to thank for this."

Father Alphonse Rose passed away in July of 2016. He warmly thanked me for remembering him and wanting to share this story. Lord, thank you for this wonderful man and his gift of faith, as well as the many faithful like Claire who cling to hope and joy among the thorns as well as the roses.

TWENTY-NINE

You Are Sitting Next to Your Wife

Mary and I pulled into the parking lot for our regular Sunday afternoon Mass at St. Ignatius parish. As we found our seats, I thought about how wonderful it was to be at the Lord's Table with so many other parishioners.

As we prayerfully participated in the Mass, I noticed a young man named Dan. His parents had come to me years earlier, sharing concerns about his troubled youth.

At their request, I met with Dan and his younger brother, trying to get to the bottom of their behavioral needs. They spoke reluctantly with me for some time, humoring me as I talked of Christ and his power to take hold of their lives if they would just allow it. I had not witnessed a positive response from Dan or his brother after our meeting, nor was there any visible fruit from the words I had shared.

I wondered how Dan had been these past few years since our talk, and I was happy to see him at Mass sitting next to a nice young lady. The Lord then abruptly interrupted my thoughts.

"Tell him he is sitting next to his wife," the Lord's voice boomed in my ears. This made me very nervous, because I knew nothing about this young lady, or about Dan at this point in his life. As I gazed at them more intently, trying to somehow draw out information about them with my eyes, a battle began in my mind.

A nagging feeling immediately crept in, warning me that I was about to do something very unusual.

I silenced the nagging voice, and in obedience to the Lord, I made my decision. After Mass, I found Dan standing in the narthex and asked if I could speak with him in private for just a moment.

He agreed, and leaving the young woman's side, he followed me a few steps away. "Dan, I have to tell you what God has just said to me," I began. "As you were sitting next to that young woman during Mass, the Lord interrupted my thoughts, and said to tell you that you are sitting next to your wife."

I quickly added, "Don't jump into anything until you pray, and talk to your parents." I certainly didn't want him to make a rash and imprudent decision based on my words alone. Dan thanked me and walked away.

The following week Dan approached me after Mass and told me that he had indeed thought about my words, and he had shared them with his mother. "Well," he started, "when I told my mom, she said confidently that this man is not usually wrong." With that, Dan said he was getting Lacey a ring.

"Oh my," I thought, at the quick decision. Then I prayed fervently, "Lord, this is hard. I don't want to do anything to misguide this young man and woman." The Lord was faithful, however, renewing me in peace as they continued to move forward with their engagement plans.

Dan and Lacey came to me many times during their engagement, and they allowed me to know them in a very special and unique way. Dan shared with me his struggles and limitations due to his severe anxiety condition, and how it produced reservations about marriage and any future commitment in general. Having suffered many of these same ailments myself, I understood clearly the physical, mental, and spiritual stress introduced into daily life.

I continued to pray with the couple and hope they could enjoy a fruitful union despite their challenges. I strongly felt the Lord intended the two of them to become one.

After postponing their wedding date more than once, Dan and Lacey finally entered into marriage and began their life together. It was amazing to witness the sacrifices they endured for one another, even early on. Lacey was extremely patient with Dan's illness, graciously forgoing even a honeymoon due to Dan's discomfort with traveling. It was no surprise that Lacey became a wonderful mother.

But it was Dan's transformation at the birth of their first child, Gabriella, that really affected me. He had been working at a garage where indecent pictures of women were hung. Having never paid the images much mind until Gabriella's birth, he suddenly was horrified by the vulgarity of the pictures. When he looked at them, all he could think was that each of those women was some daddy's little girl.

Dan and Lacey continued to welcome children into their marriage, having a child almost every two years. But things began to unravel as Dan actively pursued his dream of starting his own construction business. His past battles with crippling anxiety began to resurface with new vehemence, and I could see that he was withering. Once again, his anxiety became physically and emotionally stifling, preventing him from driving, working, and even being present for his family. Eventually, his inner fears caused him to question his decision to marry Lacey and start a family.

Lacey became deeply concerned for her husband's well being as his personal battle raged on, and their once-strong marital bond began to weaken. Along with other resources they turned to me, and together, we began working through the mountain of differences that had been building up between them.

Dan and Lacey had a solid foundation to work with, because they both were truly seeking Christ. They wanted his truth to guide every aspect of their lives. They also loved each other deeply, which was at the core of what was keeping them going.

Over the next several years, Dan and Lacey went from one crisis to another, and with them, I sought the Lord's wisdom and strength again and again. In remaining available to this wonderful couple, it became clear that Satan was trying everything to destroy them.

But despite their troubles, there were many moments of joy. They rejoiced at the births of their five beautiful children– and they celebrated when they were able to buy their own home. Finally, they praised God at the eventual success of Dan's independent dream business.

I have learned that no vocation is without trial and testing, especially those vocations ordained by God. But in Dan and Lacey, I have seen gold come out of fire. Through the constant faith they have kept burning throughout their eleven years together, many family and friends surrounding them also have been transformed, including me. God had a special plan for them, and he still does.

Lacey is a beautiful and doting mother, choosing the vocation of stay-at-home mom over her successful nursing career. She fights daily to ease the burden of her husband's anxiety in any way she is able.

Dan went from being a very troubled and self-absorbed young man with no desires for a family in his future, to taking a giant leap of faith to commit to a girl he loved and a God he trusted. Although God has not taken away his anxiety, he gives him years of reprieve.

Despite his relentless persecution, Dan has an infectious laugh, shares his love of baseball with his children, and most importantly, shares his faith. He is a living testimony of someone who follows Christ despite the darkness. Dan still says trusting it was God who spoke to him, on that day after mass, was one of the best decisions he has ever made.

> *"In this you rejoice, though now for a little while you may have to suffer various trials, so that the genuineness of your faith, more precious than gold which though perishable is tested by fire, may rebound to praise and glory and honor at the revelation of Jesus Christ."*
> *(1 Peter 1:6-7)*

THIRTY

Seek, Know, and Love God

Who am I now, after all these years and many miracles?

In some ways I am still much like the little boy in the bottom bunk of our family's Baltimore home. As I live on this earth, I too experience daily struggles. I have doubts, my family has serious medical suffering that God has chosen not to heal, and there are times I disobey God, willfully, not choosing to follow where he is leading. I am a humble sinner, in need of God's mercy and forgiveness. But I do believe in him, and that he loves me and can do all things. I am reminded daily that it is God who is in charge, and not me.

Throughout my journey, I have come across many other people who are also seeking the face of God. Some of them have fallen along the path, some have fallen on rocky ground or upon thorns, and yet others have fallen on good and rich soil and brought forth grain a hundredfold for the kingdom of God.

Those who have brought forth this grain are always watching for Christ, listening for the Holy Spirit to move, and not yielding to fear, stepping out in faith willing to be fools for the Lord.

One man I met was particularly closed to the faith, and even the pursuit of God in general. He reminded me of the seed which had fallen upon the path. He was married to a good Christian woman and heard the word of God quite often from her, but due to his unbelief and arrogance, the evil one snatched the seed away from his heart and did not take root.

One day I put forth a challenge to him—to ask for the Lord's presence directly. His eyes lit up as he looked at me slyly, accepting merely for the sake of my challenge. Then I asked him, what would God have to do to prove himself real to you? The man jokingly said, "He'd have to hit me over the head with something pretty convincing!"

I wanted to spare God the trouble and tried to do this for him myself, but I got nowhere fast. Instead, I asked the man to go someplace where he could be entirely alone and there ask God to reveal himself. I knew if he were faithful to do this with sincerity, the Lord could easily respond according to his will.

A few days later, the man sought me out at work. He was holding a large rock in his hand about the size of a softball. "What is that?" I asked.

"You're not going to believe this," he said. "According to your challenge, I hiked out to the middle of one of my farm's field, a mile away from anyone. Then, I looked up to heaven and said, 'God, if you're really here, show me.'"

Planting the large rock solidly on my desk, he recounted, "Out of nowhere, from a clear blue sky, this rock fell straight down and hit me on the head."

I burst out laughing at the thought of it. "Wow, God really got your attention, didn't he?" I said.

The moment became so special to the man that he kept the rock in a glass case with a small plaque that read, "Rock from heaven." Yet sadly, this man's pursuit of God ended there.

He was satisfied in just knowing God was real, but that was enough for him. His life became no more virtuous or morally fulfilling.

I share the miracles in this book with you, not that they should become like the rock from heaven, on display in a glass case. Rather, to see them burst forth like the grain sowed in good soil, knowing that you are being called to enjoy an authentic, personal relationship with the good shepherd, now and throughout eternity.

Ask yourself what Jesus is doing in your life, be it good or bad, and why he is allowing it to happen?

May my stories testify to the incredible love and power available in Christ. Don't be afraid to embrace God's discipline with enthusiasm, for in everything the Most High works for good with those who love him, and are called according to His purpose!

I invite you dear reader, to watch with me in prayer. Let us wait on the Lord, that together we may see God's love in every circumstance, and allow no room for Satan to induce fear and anxiety. Rather, remember he loves you, died for you, and is watching over you. Open the door to eternal communion with the only Son of God, receive him, and follow him. He is our shepherd, and we his sheep know his voice.

Because one day dear reader, we are all going to face death.

> "My sheep hear my voice, and I know them, and they follow me; and I give them eternal life, and they shall never perish, and no one shall snatch them out of my hand."
> (John 10:27-28)